ENGLISH DOLLS & TOYS

Pollock's History of
ENGLISH DOLLS & TOYS

Kenneth and Marguerite Fawdry
Researched by Deborah Brown

PRC

First published 1979 by Ernest Benn Limited
This edition published 1993 by
The Promotional Reprint Company Limited
exclusively for Bookmart Limited, Desford Road,
Enderby, Leicester, LE9 5AD
© Pollock's Toy Museum 1979

ISBN 1 85648 162 X

Printed in the Slovak Republic
51049

CONTENTS

The Authors and Publishers gratefully acknowledge permission to reproduce copyright material in this book.

Chapter II
Extract from *A London Childhood* by Angela Rodaway published by B T Batsford in 1960. Extract from *Tapioca For Tea* by Sarah Shears published by Elek Books Ltd in 1971.

Chapter IV
The autobiography of Lucy Luck, straw-plait worker originally published in *A Little of My Life* in the *London Mercury* edited by J C Squire, Vol. 13, No. 26, November 1925—April 1926 and republished by Allen Lane 1974 and Pelican 1977 in *Useful Toil: Autobiographies of Working People From 1820-1920* edited by John Burnett. Extract from a Granada Television interview William Louby, a sweet-maker's apprentice, had with John Berger in a programme called *Before My Time*, 5th June 1963. Extract from *My Early Life* by Winston Churchill published by Odhams Books Ltd, Hamlyn Publishing Group in 1930. Extract from *Floor Games* by H G Wells published by J M Dent & Sons Ltd in 1913 used with the permission of the Estate of the late H G Wells. Quote from Joyce Grenfell from *Nanny Says* by Sir Hugh Casson and Joyce Grenfell published by Dobson Books Ltd in 1972. Extract from *The Tale of Beatrix Potter* by Margaret Lane published by Frederick Warne Ltd in 1946. Milly in the Nursery extract from *Goodbye for the Present, The Story of Two Childhoods* by Eleanor Acland published by Hodder & Stoughton Ltd in 1935.

Chapter V
The description of the Lord and Lady Clapham dolls from the Sotheby & Co Sale Catalogue of 19th April 1974. Extract from *English Children's Books* by Percy Muir published by B T Batsford in 1954. Quote about Lady Jane Grey from *Boys and Girls of History* by Rhoda and Eileen Power published by Cambridge University Press in 1942 and by Dobson Books Ltd. 1965, used with the permission of The Friends of the Girls' Public Day School Trust.

Chapter VI
Quote by John Evelyn on his son from *English Children* by Sylvia Lynd, published in the *Britain in Pictures Series* by Collins 1942. Extracts from Burton's *The Anatomy of Melancholy* edited by Holbrook Jackson and Charles Lee published in the Everyman's Library series by J M Dent & Sons Ltd. 1932, 1936 and 1961.

In addition to those photographs acknowledged in the text, the authors and publishers wish to thank the following for kindly granting them permission to reproduce material in this book:

Her Majesty The Queen, Jack C. Adams, Airfix Ltd., Barratt's Photopress Ltd., Blinkhorne (Banbury), BBC, British Library, British Museum, Bodleian Library, Ray Bush, J. Stanley Clamp, Wilson Clark, Courtauld Institute, Bob Croxford, Elek Books Ltd., Fitzwilliam Museum, John Freeman, 'Games & Toys', Melvyn Gill, P Goodwin, John Gould, Mary Hillier, Hulton Radio Times Pic. Library, Illustrated London News, John Judkin Collection, Philippa Lewis, Mander and Mitchison Theatre Collection, R Metcalfe, J Moffatt, D Murdoch, National Film Archive, National Gallery, Pedigree Dolls, Yootha Rose, Tom Scott, Alistair Smith, Edwin Smith, Leslie Smith, Mrs Norman Smith, Sotheby's, John Topham Ltd, 'Toy Trader', Westminster Abbey, S de C Wheeler, Michael Wheeler, Harold White, Roderick Whitfield, Lord Willoughby de Broke.

My toys

Colin Norton, born 1969

'My favourite toy is a worm called William. He has a string on his end and I can pull him around everywhere I go. He is fluffy and he sleeps in a shoe-box in my cupboard.

'I also have ten Action Men and I have a case full of clothes for them. Sometimes I build camps for them in my garden. They have wars with my brother's Action Men.

'I have a basket full of Lego and I make trains, cars, houses, and many other things. Sometimes I make Lego cars for my Action Men.

'I also have a box full of puppets and my brother and I make puppet shows for my parents and my other brother. We have all sorts of puppets. We have a Sooty, a Kung Fu fighter, Donald Duck, Mickey Mouse and a spider on a string called Stephen.

'My dog took Tom my Teddy and bit his eyes and a bit of his face and nose off, so my Nan sewed him up.'

Matthew Evans, born 1968

'My favourite toy is my Action Man hang glider. He is put in the seat and he is towed up into the air on a string.

'My second favourite is my skate-board which is great fun to play on. If you are a good skate-boarder you should be able to do a three-sixty. Which is when you step on the back of your skate-board and do a whole circle with your front wheels in the air.

'Another toy is Scalextric, which my brother and I have great fun playing with. We had just finished making a new track. Daniel my brother put his car the Green Flash on the track and I put mine the Red Devil on the track. We had five practice laps. We lined up on the starting grid ready to go and after we had started I was in the lead and Daniel's car crashed. I was coming up to the Devil's Bend when tragedy broke out and I crashed. My brother's car overtook me and he won the race.

'This is a very exciting toy but another one which is better is Lego. One can build all sorts of things like houses, hotels and even vehicles.'

Katarina Gill, born 1968

'Tinsel Toes was my mother's teddy. She called him Tinsel Toes because she got him at Christmas and she put tinsel on his toes. He is twenty-eight years old.

'My mother has repaired his feet quite a few times. He is a honey-brown colour and has brown felt feet. Once he had glass eyes, but now he has blue wool eyes. His ears have been sewn on and repaired and he has a hole on the top of his head where the kapok is coming out.

'He is my favourite toy and is very worn, but I still love him very much.'

Daniel Webb, born 1968

'We have got an elephant and it is called Jumbo and is pink. I like punching it and I like jumping off the climbing frame on to it.

'We have five Action Men which I like playing wars with. I have got quite a lot of equipment for them. Also I have an armoured car which is green and I use it as a skate-board.

'I have also got a scale train-set; it is downstairs in our cellar. It has two trains three coaches and ten trucks and is fun to play with.

'My brother has got a money eater which is really an apple with a quarter taken out of it by a maggot which grabs your money with its fangs. I think it is a good toy.

'I have a punch ball which is coloured yellow and black stripes. What you do is tread on the black board and punch it. It is called the Olympic Junior Trainer Mark II.'

Preface

This book is designed as an introduction for the general reader. It does not attempt, therefore, to be comprehensive. It will be followed up by two volumes on the same subject which are intended as works of reference for the specialist.

Many histories of toys and dolls have appeared in recent years, but none so far which spotlights England's part in their development. This seemed, therefore, an appropriate task for our tiny museum, one of the few in England specialising entirely in dolls and toys, to undertake.

We make no apology for spilling over the edges of our subject, for neither toys nor dolls are amenable to exact definition. Moreover, while both can delight through their intrinsic beauty or ingenuity, both are no less significant for what they have meant to those who have made, sold, or played with them. Each chapter, therefore, includes memories of childhood and reference to toymakers and the toy trade.

The history of dolls and toys, in so far as it is recorded, is not a mesh of developmental strands so tightly woven that it requires the chronicler to begin in the Celtic twilight and end with to-day. We have chosen therefore to trace our story back from the familiar contemporary playroom to the shadows of the past, with the strongest focus of attention on the hundred years or so most relevant to the lover of antique toys and dolls.

This book, like so many, has incurred debts of gratitude too numerous for all to be mentioned individually. We would like however to thank especially those who have contributed their personal memories of childhood, in particular Mrs Mavis Strange, Miss Daphne Murdoch, Mr John Scupham and Mr James Heard. We are equally grateful to Mrs Beatrice Norman Smith, Miss Irene Pierotti, and Miss Peggy Nisbet for their recollections of Lucy Peck, of Charles Pierotti and of Norah Wellings respectively; to Mr Edward Newmark and Mr TV Thomas for their observations on the toy trade to-day; and to the editors of The Toy Trader, of Games and Toys, and of British Toys and Hobbies for their helpfulness in giving us access to indispensable sources.

Finally, our special thanks must go to those who helped set up Pollock's Toy Museum some twenty years ago, and to those who have been foremost in sustaining it; for the book draws much of its substance from the museum itself and is a by-product not of the study, but of the work-a-day life of an operational enterprise.

Clay marbles, Roman, *British Museum*

Colin Norton

Facing page: Katar
Daniel Webb

Rebecca Croxford with her toys, 1978

Matthew Eva

Four poster bed made by Martha-Ming Whitfield

Right: Tea-party at the Whitfields

Simon Starling

Tanya Whitfield, born 1967

'I had a little bicycle with no pedals to ride down hills, which all of our family enjoyed. It was Daddy's when he was a little boy. His mother made it.

'I was given a monkey made of rabbit fur which she made. I made myself a doll called Polly Dolly (the name comes from the book which showed how to make her, otherwise I would have named her something nicer). I still play with them a lot and I knit them clothes and make things for them.

'I have a Dutch doll and she has a large doll's house which isn't finished yet. It has three floors. I have tried to make most of the things for it myself. I made the pillow, mattress and quilt for the bed.

'I made a knitted teddy bear once but I don't really play with him. I don't play much with my plastic dolls either. I like Hollie Hobbie and rag dolls.

PS I would like a man Dutch doll because he could sleep with her without making another bedroom.

PPS But then I might need a baby Dutch doll!'

Simon Starling, born 1967

'My go-cart is made of wood. I made it about a year ago. I used some pram wheels from an old dump. My father had some planks of wood. I go down to the park where there is a very steep hill. You can go very fast on the steepest part of the hill. I went down the hill one day and the back wheel fell off so that I fell off as well. I hit my nose on a stick. If you go when it is wet you get a spray of water in your face.

'My bicycle is very old. I got it when it was third hand. When I got it it was in an awful mess. So I painted it and put a saddle-bag on it. I also put some lights and a speedometer on it.

'I ride to school on my bicycle.

'It is red with green mudguards.

'The handles are a bit rusty.'

Martha-Ming Whitfield, born 1965

'My best toy has always been my Teddy who is very old and used to belong to my Daddy when he was a little boy. All his fur has come off but I adore him and take him to bed with me every night.

'When I was about six my sister and I had a passion for dolls' tea parties. We have always played with dolls' tea-sets, mostly china ones. Our dolls' house is made out of an old mantlepiece with mirrors at the back of all the rooms. It contains a very odd mixture of dolls, even dolls to represent our family.

'Kate Norbury, a best friend of mine, and I had a session of fun when we went mad on paper dolls. We used to make them rows of clothes and hang them up on a string for all to admire. Very often we copied our own dresses and skirts.

'Another thing I enjoy playing with is roller skates. I got these myself because I wanted them so much and I have had hours of fun in the rink near our home. I also enjoy walking on stilts in the garden. I got a pair of these when I was about ten and they are still much used when children come to tea.'

Julianna Gill, born 1964

'On my seventh birthday I was given my first Sindy doll. She had dark hair and a green flowery dress. I was thrilled with her. I have a large drawer full of Sindy dolls and their furniture. My newest one is an Active Sindy. She came dressed in a white leotard and a pink ballet skirt. Her ballet shoes are also pink. Unfortunately they do not lead a very safe life as one of my Active Sindys has lost a hand and her leotard has a very large ladder in it.

'I have made five rag dolls at various times. The one I like most is my Edwardian rag doll. She is called Arabella. I made her with no help when I was nine years old. She has a complete set of Victorian undergarments and a dress-coat of lilac velvet with black velvet edging. Her hat and boots are made of chamois leather with black beads for buttons and a feather in the hat for decoration. She has her hair piled up in a large bun.

'My favourite toys are my largest teddy, a smaller teddy, an owl and a penguin. But now I have grown older I prefer craft kits. I have a paper-making kit, a perfume kit, a pin picture and a bead craft kit, a candle-making kit and a chemistry set. My favourites are the paper-making kit and the chemistry set.

'I enjoy making cardboard swords and covering them in silver foil. They all have names such as Faithful, Fearless and Dragon. I have made a shield and covered it in silver foil (this is a replica of one I have seen in the London Museum). I have made a hunting horn out of papier mâché and painted it in the right colours. It looks quite realistic.'

A tiny sample, haphazardly chosen, of children writing about their toys can prove nothing; but it can suggest. It can even demonstrate: this one demonstrates that children's concept of a 'toy' is a very elastic one. It stretches to a punchball, to stilts, to a bicycle—indeed, for one boy his toys are a go-cart and a bicycle to the exclusion of all else. A toy is whatever you enjoy handling when you're left to your own devices.

The sample also illustrates what to the educator is a truism: that what the child creates from a toy is what gives him or her satisfaction, rather than the toy itself. The most satisfying toys of all are probably those made, or part made, by the child himself; or those which (like puppets) are nothing until the child brings them to life. The time dimension can count, for children, too: teddy bears are best when matured through more than one generation, and carrying the scars of battle or accident.

The great range of activities which these mini-essays reflect are an indication of the variety of children's creative impulses rather than of any striking originality in what the toy trade offers them. This trade to-day is largely dominated by huge combines which have successively swallowed up smaller enterprises; and while these amalgamations may sometimes preserve a product which would otherwise have gone to the wall, their general effect is likely to be restrictive. The giant company will tend to reinforce success by producing more and more variations on the same theme, rather than take a plunge into the unknown: ever more Action Men conceived within a single mould of thought; ever more fashion kits for the same vacuous baby-face—this one aping a fragile sophistication, that one a cute innocence. Consider, for instance, the stories of Barbie and Sindy.

Dutch doll dressed by Martha-Ming Whitfield

Julianna Gill with rag doll made and dressed by herself

13

Barbie and Sindy

In 1945 an American company started to manufacture dolls in a converted garage. Twenty-five years later it had become one of the largest companies manufacturing and distributing toys in the world. It controls factories in Canada, West Germany, Hong Kong, Taiwan, Mexico and England (a subsidiary known as Rosebud Ltd)—quite apart from its huge plants in California. The company's name is Mattel, Inc.; the main-spring of its success a teen-age doll, Barbie, launched on the world in 1958. On the occasion of her sixteenth birthday an American journalist, Erma Bombeck, celebrated her thus:

'Sixteen years ago, naive people thought General Motors and U S Steel were keeping this country solvent. Actually it was the introduction of Barbie.

'I first met Barbie when my daughter stood in front of a counter in a department store and pleaded, "Look, Mommy, here's a doll built just like you. I want her."

'I looked at her two-inch bust, her three-inch hips and two legs that looked like two Benson and Hedges without tobacco and said, "She looks like a woman who whipped through puberty in fifteen minutes."

'"I want her", said my daughter, clutching the doll to her bosom.

'Barbie was in the house two days when it became apparent she wasn't just another doll. Barbie has needs. With the baby dolls, you could fill 'em up with water, burp them, tell them they were sleepy and sling them under the bed for a week or so.

'Not Barbie. She moved, and she needed a wardrobe to do it. Barbie went skiing ($7.95 not including ski-poles). Barbie needed lounging pajamas ($8.50). Barbie was in a wedding ($10.95).

'We eventually bought Barbie her own car ($12.95), a house ($22.95), and two friends ($5.00 each in the buff).

'One day when my husband became entangled in Barbie's peignoir drying in the bathroom (she was spending a week-end with Ken at Ohio State) he said, "What's with this doll? When does it all stop?"

'"Look at it this way", I said. "We aren't supporting just another doll, we're stabilising the economy."'

By her sixteenth birthday Barbie had acquired a platoon of family, friends,

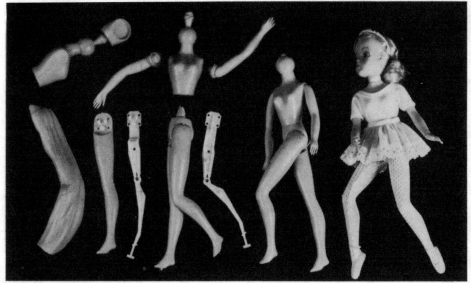

Left: Sindy in the making

friends of family, and 'licensed friends'. Friends included boy-friend, black-is-beautiful friend, and English chum; 'licensed friends' linked Barbie with the swinging world of models, movies, TV serials and Miss America. She was—is—the apotheosis of the consumer society.

Or is she? In 1978 her long reign is being challenged—by a less sophisticated, more demure younger sister, a Cinderella, made in England by Pedigree (now part of the Dunbee-Combex-Marx complex), but also in a brand-new British-owned factory on American soil. Sindy (her spelling is creative, no doubt) was designed fifteen years ago by Dennis Arkinstall; her shape and sexiness less aggressive than Barbie's, but her wardrobe and her appetite for accessories just as vast. She does not now have boy-friends—they quickly faded from the British scene—but she has ponies, camping and ski-ing equipment; she has tea-sets and furniture suites; and she has elaborate gowns to go to the ball in. Over the years her little body has changed: at first her vinyl limbs were stiff and rigid; now, thanks to her fairy godmother in the guise of designer Ian Daniels, she twists and pirouettes like a ballerina.

Over 3,500 Sindy dolls are turned out each day at Pedigree's factory in Canterbury. The torso and legs are blow-moulded from polyvinyl granules; the intricate armature of the legs is injection-moulded from a harder plastic; and a minute metal ratchet mechanism maintains the limbs in position once they are moved. The arms, with their delicate hands and fingers, are rotacast from a liquid PVC paste. In Pedigree's Hong Kong factory the little heads are made; the features are sprayed on; and nimble-fingered Chinese girls sew the innumerable accessory outfits—while in England day and night shifts work round the clock to keep up with the demand.

Dunbee-Combex-Marx make other dolls besides Sindy: a baby called First Love, a Victorian doll, a boy and girl doll inspired by Kate Greenaway's drawings, and a traditional rag doll. Their success is perhaps due in part to their relative simplicity; for as Ian Daniels (who when not designing for Pedigree is building life-size aeroplanes in his front parlour) says:

'A doll with a closed mouth is really more suitable as a plaything—for what happens when a doll is left for some time in a toy cupboard? All that food pushed down inside starts to grow mouldy and smelly fungus, and who wants that? Nowadays, too, the average mother does not want water all over the living room carpet—and one can't always send children out to play with water and their dolls in the garage or the garden. A lot of novelties are launched on the market—I've even seen quite sick things, like a pregnant doll with a baby inside—but parents today don't really want that type of thing for their children.'

Sindy is indeed not sick: far from it. She is almost indestructible, and quite irreparable.

15

Enter TV

Barbie and Sindy have enjoyed, of course, the favours of TV advertising spots to swell their sales—a field for publicity which tends to make the big enterprise bigger by remaining out of reach of the smaller. But much more significant has been TV's role in creating, or popularising, new characters which the toy trade has then taken up. By the time the doll (usually an animal with human overtones) has reached the shops, his name will already, if judgment has not faltered, be a household word. The pioneer in this field was Ann Hogarth's Muffin the Mule, presented by Annette Mills: she sold the licence to produce Muffin commercially to the firm of Lesney Products, who made an engaging little object of solid metal six inches high. Another favourite of the 1950's was Harry Corbett's Sooty, with his never-failing combination: the innocent look coupled with the infinite capacity for putting spokes in other people's wheels.

Early in the 1960s the BBC set up, as a branch of its TV Enterprises, a merchandising section to act as an agency vis-à-vis the toy trade on behalf of the copyright holder. This means that the BBC (or its commercial counterparts, which soon followed in its wake) often takes the initiative in approaching the trade—and not only the toy trade. The most striking example of TV's invasion of the retail trade was provided by the Daleks, launched on the floodtide of Dr Who's TV success. By 1965 you could buy mobile Daleks large enough for a child to get inside; stand-up inflatable Daleks; battery-operated Daleks; clockwork Daleks and mini-Daleks—not to mention Dalek slippers, playsuits, comics, jig-saws, box games, writing pads, Jelly Babies, and an 'Anti-Dalek fluid neutralizer', or water-pistol. Other major commercial successes licensed by the BBC have been the Wombles, Basil Brush, Paddington Bear and, outstandingly, Dougal from *The Magic Roundabout*, a puppet series imported from France but given a new, and very English, character by a sound track created by Eric Thompson.

Sooty, a popular TV character, licensed by his creator Harry Corbett to promote a toy xylophone

Top: Annette Mills with Muffin the Mule: Muffin, made in die-cast metal by Lesney Products Ltd in 1951, was the first toy to be marketed under licence as a result of successful TV appearances

16

The toy trade today

Abetted by TV, but with much to its credit on its own account, the toy trade in Britain is in good heart to-day. Its sheer growth over 25 years—from a product value at the factory gate of £23 million in 1950 to £234 million in 1975—is, even allowing for the fall in the value of money, impressive. The trade energetically exploited the opportunities opened up by the destruction through war of so many of the factories of Germany and Japan, giants of the international toy trade between the wars. British toy manufacturers organised their own trade association in the 1940s, their own annual trade fair in the 1950s. Outstanding among the industry's success stories are those of Lesney Products and Airfix Products Ltd.

Leslie Smith and Rodney Smith were two unrelated schoolboy friends who at the age of twelve decided that when they left school they would set up their own engineering works. In the 30s Leslie got seven years' experience with Raymond Wilson's diecasting firm; when war broke out he joined the Navy, as did Rodney, and took part in commando raids. Back at Wilson's after being demobbed, Leslie met an ex-Army sergeant, Jack Odell, who was an expert in diecasting. Then he got together with Rodney again, and they launched Lesney Products (made up from their two names) to manufacture industrial diecastings, their first factory being in an empty public house, The Rifleman, in Edmonton, North London. Let Mr TV Thomas, editor of the trade journal *British Toys and Hobbies,* carry the story on:

'The diecast scale model motor car has been a world beater for the British toy industry over a very long period. One company, Meccano, had more than a head start, for the Dinky toy was being produced in Liverpool in the 1930s—originally as station and trackside accessories to the famous Hornby trains system. However, Lesney Products & Co Ltd decided at the time of Queen Elizabeth II's coronation to use their toolmaking and diecasting expertise to make a model of the State processional Coach. This model was marketed by a well-known toy trade distributor and became a huge success. So Lesney decided to make scale models of motor cars and other vehicles for the toy trade. Then—a stroke of genius—a pack was designed for them which was a replica of an ordinary matchbox. Thus was born a trade name which to-day is known all over the world.

'The first Matchbox toys were to a smaller scale and were less expensive than

Leslie C Smith, co-founder of Lesney Products Ltd, aged 4

Early Matchbox toys and, *below,* the Aveling Barford Diesel Road Roller—the first Matchbox toy, 1953

Dinky toys. But in 1956 the Mettoy Co Ltd produced some diecast scale motor cars which were different. They were called Corgis—they were made in Wales—and they had windows! This embellishment set the pace and the competing British producers began to vie with each other to be the first to include highly detailed interior trim, opening doors and boot lids, and even 'jewelled' headlights. Since then, British producers of this type of toy have led the world.'

The Airfix Company was formed in 1939 by Mr Nicholas Kove to manufacture rubber toys filled with air; but during the war Mr Kove came to concentrate his main effort on the production of combs, which were in very short supply. His was one of the first factories in England to introduce the process of injection moulding.

In the early 1950s, new blood in the company's management set it on the path of applying injection moulding of the new plastic material polystyrene DS to the production of construction kits. First came ships, headed by The Golden Hind; then aircraft, led by the Spitfire; later veteran cars, historical figures and so on. Marketed by Woolworth's, and characterised by the accuracy of their scale modelling, these established the company's name in that branch of the toy industry. Its more recent history has been one of steady acquisitions—most notably that of Meccano and Dinky Toys—and expanded range, extending to the pre-school field, to arts and crafts kits, and much else.

In toy manufacturing today you have to be good to survive, in the longer run if not in the short; and any fair general assessment must rate the quality as well as the range of toys available today higher than at any time since mass production began. One can deplore the demise of the tin toy, yet recognise that many of those cherished today as collectors' pieces would not satisfy the exacting safety standards since imposed, with strong leadership from Britain, by international agreement. One can prefer a rag doll and a wooden yo-yo to their plastic counterparts and yet concede that the full range of plastics provides almost ideal material for children's toys—rigid or flexible; amenable to modelling of

Right: The Golden Hind—the first Airfix kit, 1954 and, *below* the Airfix Massey Ferguson Tractor Kit, 1954

unprecedented realism; durable, and above all safe. One can be cynical about the endless proliferation of Action Man's military paraphernalia and yet salute the ingenuity which has at last found the OK doll for boys. One can even argue that the over-extended wardrobe of the Action Girls and the Sindys, far from simply pandering to the acquisitive society, answers to deep-seated instincts of self-fulfilment in role-playing, and assuages, by transferring them to the fantasy world of a miniature doll, appetites too extravagant ever to be satisfied in reality. Or at least one can forbear to worry about them: they are there, like Enid Blyton, and children enjoy them.

If there has been significant progress in standards, to what is this mainly due? Edward Newmark, a director in turn of Paul and Marjorie Abbatt and of Galt Toys, attributes it to public pressure deriving ultimately from the world of education.

'The biggest change of all has occurred in the British public's awareness of toys. Until the mid-fifties toys were scarcely ever referred to in the media: in November and December a few articles would appear in the press publicising the latest new toys, and that was about all. But to-day almost all parents, during their toy buying years, have some awareness that the choice of toys is important, that toys are not just trivialities, that play value and educational value and safety are all factors to consider when buying toys. Such terms were never even associated with toys in earlier years. How has this come about?

'The most far-reaching influence at work has perhaps been, in the final analysis, the British system of Infant education, beginning at age five—at least a year earlier than in most other European countries. Aided by modern psychological knowledge and reinforced with their own experience, teachers found that young children of this age learn more by play than in any other way. To encourage and stimulate play they have needed the right sort of toys. Furthermore teachers see toys in a way parents never see them. Instead of one child with an ever changing succession of toys, they see always the same toys with a continually changing succession of children. They see therefore which toys really satisfy the child's play needs, which toys most children enjoy and go back to again and again.

'With the large sums of money spent on Primary education—and for some years after the war Britain led the world in this field—teachers could, and did, demand an ample supply of well-designed, robust and carefully thought out toys. Their demand was met by the school suppliers, companies whose business it is to manufacture or supply all the many items of furniture, equipment, and consumable goods used in school.

'The first, and for a number of years the only, supplier who could provide this sort of toy for the Infant schools was Paul and Marjorie Abbatt. The major companies in this field—The Educational Supply Association, EJ Arnold, James Galt, Philip and Tacey—were already experienced in manufacturing teaching aids for infants, however, and with this new demand coming from teachers they rapidly expanded their range of toys. Abbatt's had started as a retail shop for the general public and their school customers, though very important, did not provide the major part of their business. For the other companies it was the other way round; but when they started receiving letters from mothers asking where toys could be bought "like my little Johnny has at school" they soon realised the change that was taking place.'

Hence, in the case of Galt's a highly successful chain of shops; in the case of Arnold's and the Educational Supply Association, informative mail order catalogues widely advertised to the public. Meanwhile, the infants of the early fifties became the mothers of the early seventies and added, on behalf of their own children, to the demand for the toys they remembered from schooldays. People were caring about toys, and caring increasingly about education too; so education and toys became newsworthy, and the media joined the chorus. Simultaneously, however, there were other significant influences and personalities impinging on the world of toys.

Polythene was invented and developed by ICI Ltd. They sold the raw material for the first polythene toys, c 1950, under the trade name Alkathene

19

Yootha Rose in her workshop

Right: Toys made by Yootha Rose

Old toys for new?

The government-sponsored Design Centres in London and Glasgow, which provide information on well-designed modern products available from British firms, also mount special exhibitions and publish a series of product guides for trade buyers. The toys selected by an independent committee for inclusion in the Design Index and the Toy Buyer's Guide are not, however, in the main the products of the big manufacturing giants, but of quite small firms, many of them members of the British Toy-Makers' guild. One of the founder-members of this organisation is Miss Yootha Rose, now approaching her eightieth birthday.

Yootha Rose started her career as a child dancer, then graduated to designing sets for Sir Nigel Playfair at the Lyric Theatre, Hammersmith. Then, when war was declared in 1939, she took a job teaching art in a small country school for boys.

One bleak December day two years later, it was apparent to everyone that owing to wartime shortages the traditional Christmas tree in the village hall would be quite bare of presents. Yootha Rose decided otherwise, took out her workbag and her theatre paints, and from scraps of curtains, cushions and odds and ends of wood fabricated in three weeks a toy for every child in the village.

From that time on she never stopped. In 1946, the war being over, the London department store of Heal's put her toys on show for Christmas: within a day they were all sold, with customers queuing up for more. Carving, assembling, painting her roundabouts, her shops, her rabbit warrens, Yootha Rose yet found time to start her collection of old toys, to research into toy history and with Leslie Daiken, author of *Children's Toys through the Ages,* to found the Toy Museum now located at Rottingdean, Sussex. Her creative talent was also instrumental in setting up the first displays of Pollock's Toy Museum in 1956 and, more recently, the permanent exhibition of toys at Penshurst Place, the home of Lord de l'Isle and Dudley.

Yootha Rose's enthusiasm sparked off an interest in toy design among a new generation of art students. In 1955 John Gould, after leaving the Slade School of Art and finishing his military service, stopped by chance to look at Yootha Rose's toys and decided there and then to give up dreams of fine art and craftsman's furniture in order to concentrate on making sturdy wooden toys for Paul and Marjorie Abbatt and fleets of elegant Thames tugs for the smart new toyshops and boutiques which were opening up all over London. Twenty years later he is teaching toy design at the first course of its kind at the London School of Furniture.

Maria Wood, on leaving the Royal College of Art, abandoned the world of textile design to produce a series of imaginative cut-out-and-sew rag dolls and puppets. Brenda Cheese and Ron Fuller, whose toys fill the pages of the Design

John Gould

Left: London tug-boats, 2½ inches long, made by John Gould

Maria Wood

Left: Little Lizzie, designed by Maria Wood for Pollock's Toy Museum shop

Centre's guide, are two more of the highly-qualified art students who have turned their talents to successful toy making. Some of these, like John Spence, have found in strong, simple wooden toys an outlet for their philosophical belief in the virtue of craftsmanship and their rejection of synthetic materials and mass-production methods; others like Joy Wilcox, Louise Elliott and Sam Smith have found in toymaking a field where their nostalgia, allied with a rich and vivid sense of design, can find witty and colourful expression.

Victorian and Edwardian designs have not only been an inspiration to modern toymakers; they have kindled a new interest in the actual objects which originally embodied them. Not only has grandmama's furniture and bric-à-brac been rescued, refurbished and put to use; her toys too have been garnered from cupboard and attic to acquire the status of valuable antiques. Meanwhile the Victoria and Albert Museum, and other museums up and down the country, have been ferreting out from their storerooms dolls, games and toys which had lain there for long years unseen. We do not need to go back even to grandmama's time—a mere thirty or forty years will suffice—to find the playthings of those decades in the prestigious auction rooms of Christie's and Sotheby's. And for every collector who is attracted by their value as antiques, a hundred are captivated in part of course by simple nostalgia, but equally by the witness of their material—whether metal, wood, or woven fabric—that they belong to the pre-plastic age. The next chapter begins our journey back in time to survey them.

Benn Men—action toys made by Timothy Benn

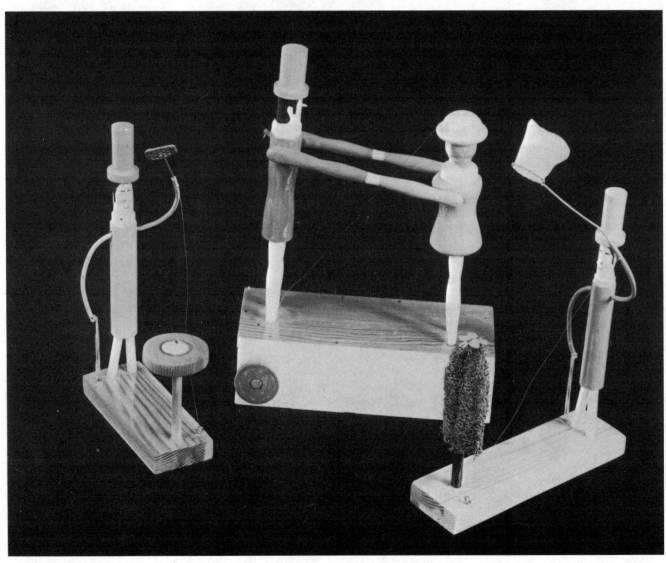

Boats by Sam Smith

Princess Elizabeth and Princess Margaret Rose, from a postcard

MAMA'S TOYS

Looking back

Childhood days between the two world wars and during the second one are still fresh in the memories of many people. Here are the recollections of three who grew up in widely differing social and financial circumstances:

Angela Rodaway, born 1918, from her book A London Childhood

"I was seven years old in the year 1925, and many things were different then from what they are now. Perhaps rich people were richer. Certainly the very poor were in great numbers, and it was to the latter class that we belonged. We were never so ill-dressed that toes came bare through our broken shoes, but rarely were we so well shod that the naked soles of our feet did not touch the pavements as we walked.'

Angela's father had lived for some time in the wilds of Canada. He fought in the First World War, then embarked on a series of unsuccessful business ventures in North London, running first a garage, then a workmen's cafe, but mostly being unemployed and living on the dole. Toys, treats and pocket money were scarce: on the way to school along the Liverpool Road the occasional penny was spent 'in a tiny "village" grocer's shop with straw on the floor and bulging sacks, millet in bunches, a smell of aniseed and vulgar sweets like tiger nuts, lotus pods, Spanish wood and coconut "tobacco", as well as the boiled sweets and halfpenny sherbet dabs that we were allowed to buy.' Gob-stoppers were forbidden by Angela's mother, who was somewhat conscious of her social superiority. A gob-stopper, as Angela explains, was 'an extremely hard, round ball that would fit into one's mouth like an egg into an egg-cup. Each was dyed in layers of very bright colour: purple, nigger, pink and poison green. You took the gob-stopper out of your mouth at intervals, sometimes in order to speak and sometimes to see what colour it had now become. Gob-stoppers were "common". I was not allowed to buy one. My only hope was to get a lick of someone else's.

'I never liked dolls—teddy bears and monkeys yes, but not my dolls. I believe I must have actively disliked them, for almost the only game I ever played with them was to hang them up round the room and hit them with a stick as I passed. The only exception to this was the baby doll, named Bobby. He had a calico trunk, very firmly stuffed with straw, and a papier maché, pock-marked face. He wore long baby clothes to hide the fact that he had no legs, and he was wrapped in a shawl because he had no arms either. The back of his head was missing too, and he had to wear a bonnet stuffed with paper. I loved him because of his terrible mutilation. That I myself had at some time been the cause of his deprivations probably did not occur to me; or perhaps it did and my exaggerated love was a form of atonement.

'One day during the summer holiday, when rain hung like cage-wire all round the house, I determined to make a golliwog. I waited until our mother was a little less busy than usual, then I asked if I could have a bit of stuff.

'"A piece of material, dear," said our mother, "not a bit of stuff", and she went to the large bottom drawer which was rather like a rag-bag and began to look through her "pieces".

'These were all classified and neatly tied in bundles. But I could not make a golliwog of Indian muslin and I did not want one with flowers all over him, like a skin disease. Even a golliwog could not look as funny as that.

'In the end my mother lost patience, brought out a piece of sheeting and, shutting the drawer, said, "Then you may have that. It's all there is".

'"But it's white!" I exclaimed hopelessly.

'"It's a lovely piece of material", answered our mother. "Pure linen and very strong."

'My father said, "I've heard of white negroes in Africa. They're called albinos and they have red hair."

'The idea of making an albino golliwog was not unattractive, especially when my mother offered me an old woollen glove which I could unravel to make beautiful, curly red hair.

'When he was finished, he looked quite presentable. He had two pink glass buttons for eyes and his hair was brilliant.

'Outside the family the first person to see "Alby" was the sweep. "What an extraordinary thing! "he exclaimed. "What is it?"

'"It's a golliwog", I answered. "He's an albino."

'"A what!" His mouth flew open and he roared with horrible, excluding, grown-up laughter. He laughed so much he could hardly stand up and had to hold on to the railings. He laughed until the tears came into his eyes and made little pink runnels in the soot on his cheeks.

'From then onwards Alby's life was full of love, devotion and many disastrous adventures. He was shipwrecked in a muddy pond all slimy with duckweed, dropped into a pan of boiling jam, and finally sent off, in the pocket of mother's coat, to be dyed to the last shred of his stuffing a deep mourning black'.

Daphne Murdoch, born 1934

Daphne Murdoch was five years old on a bright September morning in 1939 when the first air raid warning sirens shattered the peace of the quiet suburban road in Sutton where she lived. The following year, as the air raids on London grew in intensity, Mrs Murdoch shut up the little house and decided to move to the country, living as near to her husband as his different army postings permitted.

Daphne's toys were packed away in the attic. She was a much loved and cherished only child. Her grandmother and aunts had given her china dolls and toys they had treasured from their own childhood. Her father had made her a large dolls' house and, when he was stationed at Dover, aeroplanes and dolls' furniture with wood salvaged from bombed-out houses.

'Most of my toys were left at home,' says Daphne, 'and so weren't played with much. Between six and nine years old I had construction toys, and great favourites of mine were the cut-out doll dressing books. I played with them for hours, and they were easy to pack. Of course I had skipping ropes and marbles—some of these were ball bearings, as glass ones were hard to come by.

'I used to spend my pocket money in Woolworth's, either buying farm animals or soldiers. I was also at this time given "Mary", a German china doll, by one of our neighbours, and told she was eighty years old then. She had no wig, and the only one we could obtain was the short blond one she still wears.

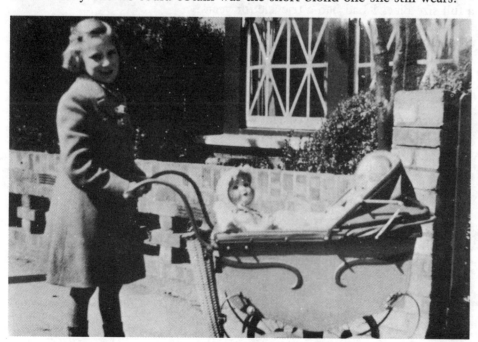

Daphne Murdoch outside her home in the Second World War

Daphne Murdoch's tea party

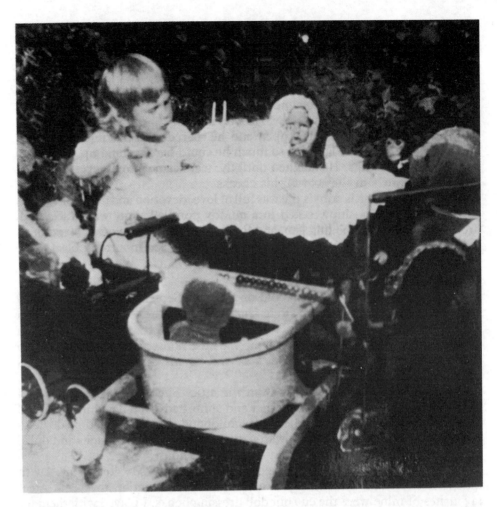

'When I was nine we moved to Halifax in Yorkshire, as the doodlebug VIs were bad at home. We stayed with a lady who had a brother fifteen years younger than herself, and together we played with cutouts from pre-war catalogues in shops made from cardboard boxes. I made dolls, from clothes pegs—the old fashioned kind—, and in a local shop you could buy small plaster dolls for sixpence, which you coloured yourself. I was very lucky at this time to be bought a full-size bike. I had had a tricycle for years.

'I was also a great reader, and Mum bought me many Girls' Annuals—mostly from jumble sales. Of course I had some new books, but paper was scarce. I was (and still am) very fond of jigsaw puzzles, and I had loads of them, getting harder as I grew older.

'We had a school teacher billeted on us while her husband was in the RAF. He made a wooden doll and she dressed it, and also made me a clown on a stick.

'On returning home I played a lot with my farm, using the bricks as fences, or building arches and bridges. For the first time really, the dolls came into their own as I tried my hand at dressmaking for them—not very well I may add. I also started to modernise my dolls' house, but was really getting too old for it.

'About the last toy I was given was the plastic circus from Woolworth's, but I never really played with it, as I was too busy with homework and Brownies, and later Guides.'

So Daphne's toys were packed away once more in boxes and put in the attic; and there they remained until 1977, when they were taken out and put on show at Pollock's Toy Museum, to play a small part in Queen Elizabeth II's Jubilee celebrations.

Doll with composition head made by Dura Porcelain Co during the Second World War

Cut-out paper dolls sent to Daphne Murdoch from USA during the Second World War

Left: One of the first toys in hard plastic sold by Woolworth's

Furniture made for Daphne Murdoch's monkey by her father, from wood taken from bomb sites

Right: Paper cut-out of the Maginot Line, showing French and British soldiers

Bottom: Chad Valley vehicles 1938-48, *Geoffrey Baker Collection*

Facing top: Aeroplanes made by Daphne Murdoch's father From the Triang catalogue 1937

Facing below: Soldiers bought by Daphne Murdoch at Woolworth's *Inset:* Paper cut-out ATS girl

Below: HMS Victory—a wartime jigsaw

From the Triang catalogue 1937

Right: James Heard, aged 18 months

James Heard, born 1943

'The first toy I ever bought for myself was a Massey-Harris manure spreader with working parts. I had seen it the week before in the window of Warden's toyshop, and returned with 3s 9d to acquire this red painted Dinky toy that was to become the star of my collection of battered second-hand vehicles. I always wanted the tractor that should have pulled my manure spreader, but I never saw one for sale or swop. It was the same with my military Dinkies, for I had a reconnaissance car and a six-wheeled wagon with a spare tyre fixed to the driver's door, a model searchlight, and a gun which fired matchsticks—but I never had a tank.

'Growing up just after the war meant that toys were either home made or handed down from a relative or neighbour, for playthings were as carefully repaired as socks were darned. Because their construction was sturdy and the materials basic it was possible for the least dexterous dad to mend a broken toy—whereas to-day the ubiquitous plastic defiantly refuses to be glued, pinned or taped. I must confess my father was not very practical and was anyway busy with Mother running a preparatory school for boys. I was in the care of a nanny and her husband, the school carpenter Claude, who produced some superb home-made toys in his corrugated iron workshop—the best was a sword and shield with a leather strap. Being an only child, I fought most of my skirmishes with imaginary knights who turned out to be sturdy willow trees, but a wooden sword could always be repaired. Claude also made me some stilts, but I could never manage them nor understand the need to be so tall.

'An early trauma was the dreadful slaughter of Piglet and Penguin, two stuffed animals who came with me to the isolation hospital when scarlet fever struck. Nurses and, very occasionally, parents looked in through a large glass window: only Piglet and Penguin kept me company. In the confusion of leaving that hateful place I lost track of my cloth friends. They had been burnt alive to destroy their germs. During a later bout of illness I was presented with a Teddy Bear, but I was too old to love it much—he too might be destined for an equally nasty end, and he was not home made. Soft toys have more personality if they have been made from scraps of material; but trains, cars and guns are best left to the toy manufacturers.

32

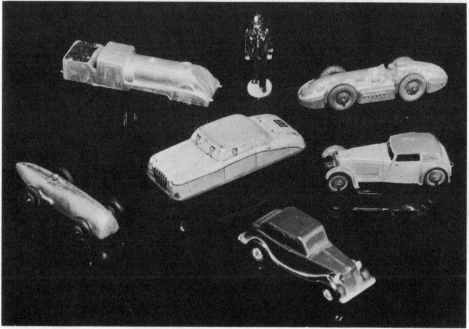

Steamrollers, *Pollock's Toy Museum*

Left: Cars, *Pollock's Toy Museum*

Below: From Britain's catalogue 1935

'I loved my cream and red Triang pedal car, specially ordered for a birthday from Kendall Milne's in Manchester. Such luxury toys could only be found at large department stores in the 1940s, and the usual stock of the local toyshop would be largely made up of cheap items: glass divers who descended inside a bottle of water when the cork was touched, or two tiny metal dogs mounted on magnets to make them fight and frolic. Later, the Coronation provided the toy makers with an incentive to produce more cheap toys: I remember Dean's Coronation Cut-out story book, and embossed scraps of the Queen's head. Looking back I realise I was one of the scissors-and-paste generation, who was most happy when doing something with paper; making hectographs to duplicate my toy theatre programmes, fiddling with the John Bull printing set, begging

33

for the cut-outs on the back of the cornflake packet, or crying with frustration over the origami instructions in the Rupert Bear Annual.'

Angela Rodaway's childhood, though a bare couple of generations away, seems more than half-way back to Dickens. Hers is a world in which an abundance of toys was the privilege if not of the few, then certainly of the minority only of children. And for those born, like Daphne Murdoch and James Heard, in the thirties or forties, even if their circumstances were much easier, there was a good deal of the home-made and the make-do-and-mend about their world of toys. The contrast with to-day appears striking; yet the toy trade in the days of mama's childhood—between 1925 and 1950—in fact embodied in embryo all the features we have found to characterise it to-day. It was in the 1930s that the ideas were germinated which later made 'child's play' a phrase for educators, then parents, to ponder; and it was the 1930s which saw the earliest applications of synthetic fibres to toy manufacture. Foreshadowing the huge multi-national toy empires of the 1970s was the hitherto unexampled growth of domestic firms such as Lines Brothers and Chad Valley; and foreshadowing TV's impact on the toy trade from the 50s onwards was the cinema's in the 20s and 30s.

Pop and Dismal Desmond. As a newspaper strip cartoon character, Pop lasted a record forty years, with 12,000 strip appearances

Below: From the Triang catalogue 1937

Mary Pickford and after

Early in 1922 Mary Pickford, the celebrated Hollywood film star, decided to invest over 25,000 dollars in setting up a factory to manufacture dolls in her own likeness. 'This represents my first venture into any commercial field not connected with motion pictures' she explained, 'and I want to be able to give the product my personal attention, which is the reason I am so anxious to establish the factory here in California.'

Although it seemed at first quite a simple thing to turn out a miniature likeness of the star, it quickly developed into a baffling problem. Nearly three quarters of a year was spent in trying to obtain a suitable reproduction. The services of eight artists and sculptors were employed, but the task was not accomplished until Christian van Schneidan, the most famous Scandinavian artist in America, was commissioned to do the work.

Sixty different models were made, and also one life mask which almost turned into a death mask, as Mary Pickford was nearly suffocated in the process; and her face was so badly bruised by the weight of the plaster that for several days it was impossible for her to appear before the camera.

The resulting Mary Pickford doll was one of the first of a long line of promotional dolls and toys inspired by the popular stars of the silver screen. The list grew year by year: Felix the Cat, Charlie Chaplin, Baby Betty, Jackie Coogan, Buster Brown, Shirley Temple, Mickey Mouse and all the Walt Disney creatures. Mr Edward Davis, director of Walt Disney Mickey Mouse Ltd in Wardour Street, London, was endlessly busy negotiating manufacturing licences for every conceivable type of toy, game or object. Film merchandise was big business indeed.

There was money, too, to be gained from dolls or toys based on well-known books, newspaper cartoon characters, or people in the public eye like the little

Popeye, the Sailor Man was a popular film cartoon of 1936. This doll was made by Dean's Rag Book Co, *Mary Hillier Collection*

35

princesses, Elizabeth and Margaret. Advertising promoted the product: the product in turn promoted the book, personality or institution from which it derived.

Promotional toy production assumed a mass market, and catering for a mass market required mass production methods—which were anyhow proving necessary in order to survive. The multitude of small firms that had come into being in the First World War were gradually eliminated as import restrictions were lifted at the end of it. They were unable to meet the competition of foreign firms. Only the large and efficient survived—by becoming still larger and still more efficient.

Lines Brothers

One of the outstanding successes was that of Lines Brothers. Walter Lines and his two brothers decided on demobilisation not to return to the family business where they had worked since their schooldays preparing cowtails and horsehair for rocking horses. They acquired large premises near a wharf in the Old Kent Road and showrooms in the City; and organised one of the first up-to-date mass production lines for rocking horses, dolls' houses, dolls' prams, fairy cycles, scooters, pedal cars and large pull-along engines. Their drive and organising skill were such that by 1925 they were building what was then the largest toy factory in the world out in the fields of Merton, not far from South Wimbledon railway station.

Very soon after, more factories were built or acquired in Birmingham and in Wales to produce flying scale-model aircraft, miniature clockwork toys and Pedigree dolls with their accessories: dolls' clothes, eyes, wigs and shoes. Lines bought up paint-making works to ensure a high-quality finish to all their products, and engaged chemists and other scientific research staff to supervise technical operations and to develop new ideas. The famous triangle trade mark in the end appeared on almost every kind of toy imaginable.

The one notable exception was guns: Lines did not make any kind of warlike

Right: Triang gyro-cycle, 1938

36

weapon. By a strange coincidence, however, during the Second World War the Lines Brothers' factories were almost wholly engaged in developing and producing the Sten gun, a cheap, mass-produced, easily fired machine gun which became a vital part of the equipment of the Allied forces.

Of all the forty or so companies and subsidiaries that made up the Lines empire, perhaps none was more dear to Walter Lines than Hamley's in Regent Street. As a young boy he had made weekly visits to the shop, perched up beside the driver of his father's horse-drawn delivery van. Not only did he enjoy the ride from North London to the centre, but he had also his own private arrangements to make with Mr Hamley for the sale of the dolls' house furniture he made after school hours. In 1925, when financial difficulties threatened to close down the shop, Walter Lines made his first venture into the retail trade by very willingly buying up the greater part of Hamley's shares.

Chad Valley

The pattern of growth and expansion into ever larger units of production followed by Lines Brothers found parallels in other toy firms. Chad Valley Ltd grew from a tiny printing works to one of the largest manufacturers of soft toys and games by a continual process of more and more self-sufficiency.

Joseph Johnson and his brother Alfred set up their printing works in George Street Parade, Birmingham in the year 1860. Their main business was in printing labels, headed stationery and so on. They prospered and in 1897 moved to larger premises at Harborne, in the Chad Valley, where to printing they added the manufacture of boxes, board games and jigsaws. Then in another factory, close to a railway siding and a timber yard, they started to produce draughts, chessmen, dominos and other pieces for their board games. The firm expanded by buying up one company after another: the Wrekin and the Issa works for soft toys and dolls, the Wellington works for rubber and metal toys, the Tan Bank factory for teddy bears; while yet another firm, making metal boxes, was bought up and switched to toymaking. Later Kenneth Horne, a famous wartime BBC

From the Triang catalogue, 1937

Left; Triang lorries, 1938, *Pollock's Toy Museum*

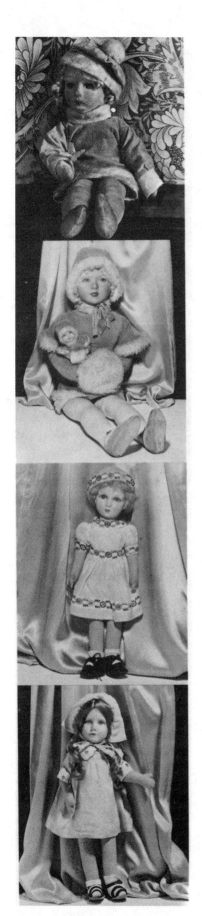

Dean's Rag Book dolls

personality, was appointed a director when his family wood-working business, Roberts Brothers of Gloucester, was absorbed into the Chad Valley empire.

Meanwhile in London the other giant of the soft toy trade, Dean's Rag Book Company, was turning out a succession of Felix the Cats, Dismal Desmonds, Blinkums and Dinkums, Pip Squeak and Wilfreds, and other cuddly character dolls. But the most distinctive contribution to the soft toy industry was being made by a former Chief Designer of the Chad Valley Company, Norah Wellings, who left them in the mid-twenties to set up on her own account.

Norah Wellings

Norah Wellings was able to leave the business side of her enterprise in the hands of her brother Leonard, concentrating herself on design and production; and already by 1927 her Trade Fair exhibits were being lauded in the journal *Games and Toys* as outstandingly successful. These exhibits, which she named Cora dolls, had felt faces, glass eyes, moveable joints, and wigs of real hair; their design, while clearly influenced in style by the work of the popular children's book illustrator Mabel Lucy Attwell, achieved a certain artistic distinction and revealed, in such dolls as Lady Golfer and Caddie, a delicate, faintly ironical humour. Moreover, the dolls were invariably technically well made, and reasonably priced for the middle class market. Within a few years their designer was being presented to Queen Mary, a notable doll enthusiast and collector.

Through the 1930s Norah Wellings continued to expand her range, with Dutch boys and girls, Chinese girls, Irish and Scots character dolls; a series of animals—elephants, birds, dogs, monkeys; 'novelty' dolls: clowns, pirates, black dolls; and so on. Best known of all, however, were the Sailor Boys made for the Cunard Steamship Co as mascots for transatlantic and cruise travellers; and in the Second World War, Harry the Hawk, a mascot for the RAF.

Peggy Nisbet, who knew Norah Wellings personally and continued her tradition of soft toy making after her retirement, has written of her: 'Norah Wellings's dolls were her life. Into them she put much of herself, and she felt they were her family. This may be why her own creations seemed to have so much more character than other not dissimilar dolls produced by larger manufacturers of the same period.

'Two of her creations I particularly admired were a pair called simply Man and Woman: they were beautifully executed and there was a great deal of detail in the costume. The faces were in pressed felt, and the man's was a lovely piece of characterisation.

'Another outstanding doll had a pressed black velvet face with a large beaming smile, glass eyes and a black mohair wig piled high on her head. She wore large white earrings and strings of coloured wooden beads—a most enchanting little figure.

'Norah Wellings's dolls were ideal for small children. In most cases even the bodies were made of velvet, so they were soft to the touch, cuddly and lovable; but such was their appeal that adults, too, fell in love with them. All her dolls had firmly sewn on labels, so they were easily identifiable.

When Norah Wellings retired, Cunard asked Peggy Nisbet if her company would be prepared to make similar mascots for them. 'I had always had an affection', she relates 'for all Norah Wellings creations, so I got in touch with her and asked whether, as she herself had ceased production, she would have any objection to our making them, either under licence or under some arrangement with her. She said no, she would like no one better to make sailor boys for the shipping lines, but would I please not ask her for her patterns or techniques. These were, she said, so much part of herself and of her brother that she could not hand them over to anyone else as it would be like parting with part of herself. But by all means I could make her sailors if I could develop them myself. As for fees and royalties, she wanted nothing. She merely wished me every success with them.'

Norah Wellings's Sailor doll, made for selling on board Cunard's SS Orontes

Advertisement in *Games and Toys* for Norah Wellings's Norene dolls, 1936

Top left: Norah Wellings doll, dark-brown velvet, 1929

New materials

As the toy trade organised itself into ever larger manufacturing and marketing units, there was intensive experiment to find the materials most amenable to mass production methods. In 1935 Mr Charles Pierotti made his last wax doll in the basement of his house in the Goldhawk Road, West London, and retired from the business. A single firm in the Potteries continued to turn out a few china doll's heads, but the day of the china and the wax doll was long since past. Every manufacturer was experimenting with more and more varied mixtures of plaster of Paris, sawdust and resin in order to produce dolls' heads cheaply and quickly. Rubber, bakelite, and early forms of hard, plastic type materials made from cellulose powders and compounds were tried out, often with rather crude and unpleasant results.

Mr Hilary Page, a distinguished toy designer who gained a large following by his broadcast talks *Playtime in the First Five Years*, wrote in 1939: 'I experimented with all sorts of materials, but was unable to find any paint or enamel which suited my purpose. I turned to the bakelite range but was not satisfied even with this material. Eventually I found a combination of materials which proved to be entirely satisfactory for my purposes.

'We have called this material Bri-plax, and I consider it is miles ahead of any material ever previously used in the manufacture of toys for babies and young children. It is available in a very attractive range of colours. It is completely hygienic, can be washed indefinitely with soap and water, and boiled for short periods. It is strong and durable. It is non-inflammable. It is light in weight. Even with constant sucking, gnawing and biting it is impossible for a young child to remove the slightest trace of either the colour or the material. Within the last few months I have produced five really practical toys in Bri-plax, and every one of these is selling very well indeed, and is bringing me a constant flow of letters of appreciation from mothers'.

A week after Kiddicraft Ltd had announced the appearance of the new Bri-plax rattles, building beakers and pyramid rings, war was declared; and along with all the other toy manufacturers in Britain they turned their attention to more essential things. Only a few elderly workers were left tucked away in factory corners producing a small range of games, jigsaws and other simple toys.

Plastics, nylon and other synthetic materials were put to more and more uses, until in the post-war years they became almost the basic materials of the toy industry. Mr Hilary Page sounded a warning note when in 1948 he quoted from a mother's letter begging him not to make any of those 'darn plastic toys. I am always,' she said, 'picking up the pieces and wiping tears away when they break. They are beautiful to look at, but rarely last two days, and so many women I know are refusing to buy them any more.'

Hilary Page answers these complaints by stating: 'The material is not at fault, but the design is all wrong. Manufacturers have endeavoured to cheapen the price of plastic toys by using less and less material, until the resulting toys are far too fragile to stand up to the hard use they will get in homes, nurseries and schools.'

The Abbatts

Two people who reacted strongly against the shoddiness and unsuitability of many toys for young children were Paul and Marjorie Abbatt. They would only consider selling a plastic toy, or any other toy for that matter, after Paul Abbatt had jumped on it to see if it would break.

The Abbatts had very decided, and at that time very revolutionary, ideas about toys for growing children. Both had trained as teachers, and both believed passionately in the educational value of toys and play in a child's development. They were much interested in the pioneer work of Montessori and Froebel, and above all in the books and educational theories of Susan Isaacs. They had spent their honeymoon in 1930 touring Europe to study theory and practice in the field of infants' play. The toys and apparatus used in Viennese kindergartens impressed them particularly, and on their return they held a small exhibition of the toys they had collected in Europe and the USA. This aroused so much interest that they ended up by producing a catalogue illustrated by the sculptor John Skeaping, and starting a mail order business. The demand was such that they eventually opened a shop in Wigmore Street which for thirty years catered for what the Sunday Times called 'all the terribly sensible, terribly enlightened parents.'

So while the toy industry as a whole, with some distinguished exceptions, was busy tempting the public with mainly catchpenny novelties, teachers and parents were beginning to search for the simple and the sturdy. The seeds of a new movement were sown which was to reach full fruition after the war, when the hessian sack full of plain wooden offcuts became fashionable and the label 'educational' almost a necessary passport to success in the toy trade.

In December 1963 The Sunday Times, reporting an interview with Lines Brothers, stated: 'They deny that they go in for gimmicks such as hula hoops and yoyos. "We cater," they said, "for all tastes. Our aim is to provide the best of all types of toy, from the educational to the novelty."

'Mr Kenneth Furnival, a director of Lines, when asked for his definition of a toy, said: "A toy is an imitation of an actual article used by an adult." With this, his first reply, he played himself right into the hands of the enemy. Then he half retrieved himself by adding: "A toy must also develop imagination." Finally he said: "The finest toys are bricks." He was home and dry. The educationalists would speak to him again.'

40

An Edwardian beauty's publicity photograph

GRANDMA'S TOYS

Looking back

Mavis Strange, born 1895

Mrs Mavis Strange, looking back over eighty years, remembers standing at the age of five in a corner, crying, her head pressed against the wall.

' "What is it, dear?" "The Queen is dead." "Now don't be silly. She was very old and you've never seen her." '

'A few years later Edward VII came to Birmingham to open a school, and I begged mother to take me with her. A large drapery store had offered seats to their best customers. We sat for hours in the hot, uncomfortable shop front, and then in a flash the King went by—a fat, paunchy old man in a top hat, with a perfectly ugly face.

'From that time on I played Cromwell in our unending games of Roundheads and Cavaliers. We used to dress my little sister up as a princess, perch her on top of a cupboard, and then forget all about her while we fought our valiant battles using Father's bayonet from the Franco-Prussian War, and penny pistols with caps.

'We did not have many toys. I remember a diabolo craze, bowling a hoop, and playing with a golliwog and a family of ½d wooden dolls who lived in a beautiful dolls' house Father made for us. He had worked at it in the basement, keeping it mysteriously covered in a dust sheet. The furniture was marvellously contrived, and the grates had been made from the lids of carbolic tooth powder, cut in half.

'My first china doll was called Curly-Locks. I must have been four or five years old when I was given it, and I spent all that Christmas Day nursing it in the night nursery, with the curtains drawn, as I thought she must have been tired after her long journey.

'That same Christmas my sister stole my tiny Dutch doll called Midget, like the one in the Golliwog books, and when she was found out she threw it in a temper out of the nursery window, where it was lost in the snow. Father, who was rather puritanical and strict with us, picked up the beautiful walking doll which had just been given to my sister, and threw it in the fire. I can still see the springs inside it writhing in the flames.

'My sister had a doll called Maudie Morgeana. Its wax face started to peel, and my sister used to sit scraping at it with her finger nails. It had huge, bulbous

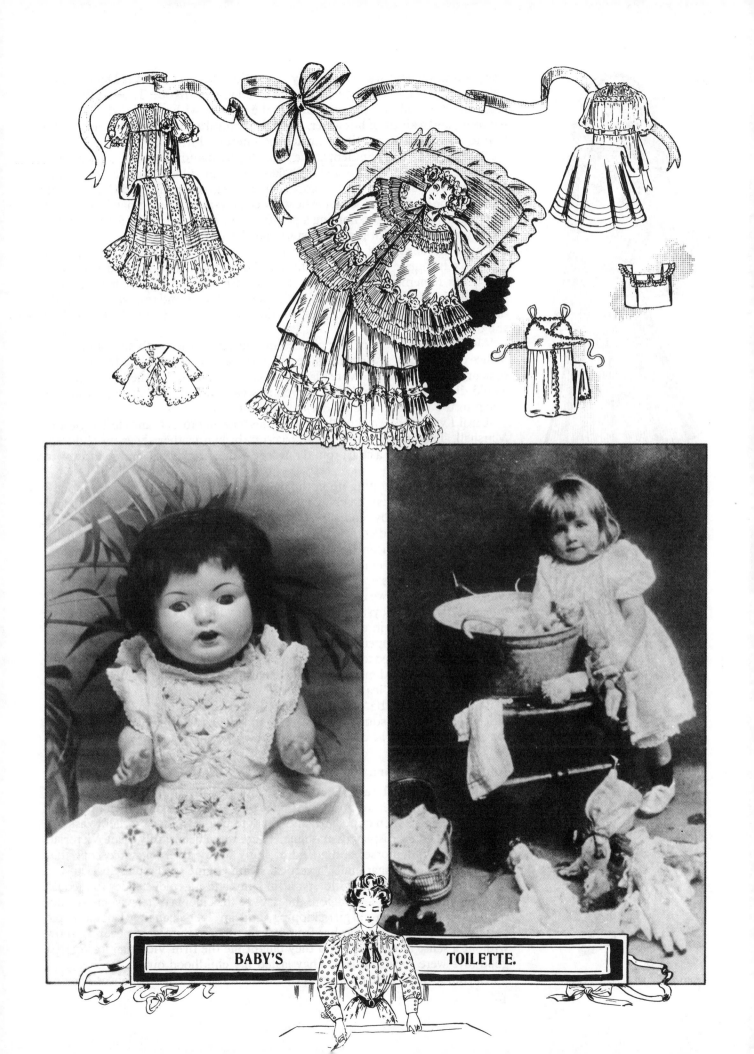

BABY'S TOILETTE.

From *The World of Dress* 1904

eyes, and in the end was a hideously ugly thing. My last doll was Dora Areate, given to me when I was twelve after I had had my tonsils out. The family doctor came and did us all in turn, on a table in the nursery with just a bowl to wash his hands in, and a kettle of hot water. I kept Dora until a few years ago, when I gave him to an American gentleman who was interested in dolls.

'We had few entertainments. We went to the pantomime, and to see Peter Pan, and dear Frank Benson in a Shakespeare play. Once a year Nurse would escort us to a matinée of the Bioscope, which was given in dirty old Curzon Hall. We sat in the best seats—sort of little wooden pews; and a gentleman in a tail coat and bright yellow gloves, holding a pointer, showed us the salient features of the scenery displayed with jerks and starts on the screen.

'Nurse used to read aloud, in a harsh, crackly Birmingham voice, from *Stumps,* a favourite book, about a little girl of my own age. We read at an early age: I can remember spending my 1d pocket money on *Books for the Bairns,* published by WT Stead. All the Nesbit books were read and re-read and, greatly daring, I wrote a letter to her. This was the start of a friendship which lasted till she died.

'Mother made most of our clothes in Liberty fabrics with smocking, on a Willcox and Gibbs sewing machine. Children always wore white frocks with a pink or blue sash. I never wore black: I longed to do so, and wished that someone would die and that I would be allowed to wear black. I even dreamt of myself dying in the night and being decked out in funeral black.

'Until I was nineteen, I could pick daisies with my toes, thanks to Dowie and Marshall. They made square-toed, lace-up, brown leather shoes for children. Mother used to draw a chart round our feet with a prickly pen and send away to London for them.

'I can remember getting up in the morning on cold, dark winter days; one's horrible underclothes—thick wool combies; prickly, starchy drawers; and sometimes blue woolly bloomers, blacked ribbed stockings and a liberty bodice made of white quilted cotton, with shoulder straps with buttons on for growth, and suspenders with an ugly bone button; a flannel petticoat and a starchy cotton one with lace embroidery.

'And of course hats or tam o' shanters outdoors, except during the holidays in North Wales, where we raced over the hills in blue knickers, or Scotch kilts and blue fishermen's jerseys, our hair flying in the wind. Mother was considered to be very "advanced" in allowing this.

'When I was a flapper, that is to say, when we wore our hair tied back with a big black bow, we used to go roller-skating—but always in a party, never alone. I was taken to Paris and made to wear my hair in a knot. Mother said, "You won't learn French, but at least you'll learn to wear a hat properly."

'I never wanted to be "grown-up." I was sorry for them, poor things, in their hideous clothes and squeezed-in waists, and their frizzy hair, tight shoes and long skirts. Then 1914 came and one "grew up", like it or not.'

John Scupham, born 1904

The first toys that I remember were, quite literally, out of my reach. Too precious or too dangerous for a little boy to play with on his own, their home was a high built-in kitchen cupboard, and I had to beg my older brother to ask my mother if he could display them to me. There was a beautifully made Victorian waggon with four horses and a load of shiny little barrels; a stereoscope that showed views of Niagara falls; a vertical steam engine with a piercing whistle; and a truly magic lantern with a paraffin lamp and ingenious slides that could show moving pictures long before the days of the cinema or television—a train running over a bridge, a girl skipping, and an ever-changing kaleidoscopic pattern. Brought by my mother from her own home they were never on show without a sense of occasion, and they taught me the firm Victorian lesson that good toys were meant to last. They lasted my childhood out.

'Of course there were minor toys that made no claim to permanence. The tiny

46

From Gamage's catalogue, 1913

Left: From *Punch Almanac*, 1903.
Enthusiastic Little Model. 'Oh,
that *is* pretty! There's me and
there's my Dolly! Oh, and now I
see why you made me wear a
blue sash and my Dolly wear a
pink sash!.'
Artist. Why?
E.L.M. 'Why, because now
people can see which is me and
which is my Dolly!'

Mavis Strange, aged 2. 'We always
wore hats or tam-o'-shanters.'

market town at the foot of the Lincolnshire Wolds that was our world before the coming of the motor car had its own high street toyshop. Rich with my Saturday penny, my Tuesday penny, or with both together, I used to set out for an eager survey of Mr Fieldhouse's stock in the days when a penny would buy a monkey on a stick or a celluloid baby in a bath; a sheet of transfers or a sheet of scraps; a helmeted soldier or a weighted doll—a "kelly" who wouldn't lie down; a magnet or a handful of marbles. There used to be five kinds of marbles then; perhaps there still are. "Trats" were small white matt-surfaced marbles ringed with coloured line. "Commonies" were larger marbles of plaster, painted a single colour. "Gingers" were the glass marbles from the necks of broken ginger-beer bottles. "Glassies" were of clear glass with a coloured spiral running through. "Blood alleys", the aristocrats of the game, were indeed made of a creamy marble, with a crimson vein, and in the strict currency of the street games that I later learnt to play each blood alley was worth sixteen trats.

'Christmas, and Christmas alone, was the time for new toys of consequence. It was heralded for all of us—two boys and two girls— by the eagerly awaited plop through the letter-box of Gamage's inexhaustible mail-order catalogue. For me, when I was old enough to pore over it for myself, it conjured up romantic visions of huge model yachts, train sets that would fill our biggest room, and resplendent regiments of artillery equipped with cannon which could fire rubber shells, and not mere matchsticks, like mine. But these, I knew, were beyond me. The real fun lay in the discovery of treasures beyond Mr Fieldhouse's resources which my mother might realistically be expected to order. There would be surprises for the whole family: a clockwork bear that turned head over heels to be a nine days' wonder, a box of wire puzzles, a wig or box of grease paints to enrich the dressing-up box full of old hats, ladies' veils, and faded finery for the family charades that were the highlight of all our Christmases. But for me, which would she choose of all the coveted items I had marked: the whistle guaranteed to decorate a friend's face with charcoal when he blew it, the dummy camera that would fire a snake at him, the spring gun that would fire arrows tipped with rubber suction pads, or an extraordinary new kind of top? For many years tops were my favourite toys; hollow metal humming tops with spiral push-in activators or with separate spring winders from which they could be suddenly released; magnetic tops which could persuade steel snakes to wriggle round their spinning points; gyroscopes that could walk the string tightrope or stand immobile on little towers; outdoor tops, with four shapes to choose from at Mr Fieldhouse's for a penny each; and the little tops that we used to make with matchstick spindles and cardboard discs, and colour with crayons so that they showed new and surprising and beautiful colours as they spun.

'Making them was one of our regular occupations whenever the weekend or the school holidays brought the keen pleasures of settling down for a day so rainy that there was no prospect of going out. A noisy, combative, close-knit family group, we shared our indoor toys and games, and endlessly competed with each other. We had indoor skipping competitions, and painting competitions, and building competitions with our mother as patient referee until even her patience gave out and she imposed on us a silence competition. It was only on rainy days that it was worth while to set out our paintboxes and to embark, not on bold creative pictures in the modern mode, but on the meticulous colouring of the pictures in Grimm or Hans Andersen, *The Rose and the Ring* or *The King of the Golden River*. Then, too, was the time to unpack the greatly treasured box of German bricks of artificial stone, red, yellow and slate blue in many shapes and sizes, with its pattern book of houses and chateaux, bridges and churches, but with its mute invitation to wild architectural fantasies. At the end of the day all the bricks had to be ritually packed in the only possible way into the strong wooden box with a sliding lid, and that was part of the fun.

'Or perhaps our fancy would run to competitive games; to Tiddlywinks on the short-pile carpet, or Snakes and Ladders, or Beggar my Neighbour varied by card-castle building, or Happy Families. They were foreign families, and I still

48

see clearly the well-thumbed Miss U No Sum Sing of Japan, and Mr Drifigs, the Terrible Turk. And as we grew older, and kept open house for all our friends, the greatest pleasure of all was to let an extra leaf into the big dining-room table, and to lay across it the heavy folding bagatelle board—another Victorian survival— or to fetch out the double-parchment-sided racquets (not bats) for the game that was still rightly called ping-pong.

'On fine holidays we spent very little time indoors, and as the era of whips and tops, of hoops and marbles drew to a close my own indoor occupations were more and more pressed into the service of my outdoor pursuits. In those days my constant and never-to-be-forgotten guide was Arthur Mee's *Children's Encyclopedia*, bound up from its monthly issues, and all the more interesting because you had to chase your quarry of the moment, whether poetry or puzzles, through all of its stout eight volumes. ''The next section of things to make and things to do is on page 1467'', it would announce, and there on page 1467 would be clear and cheap instructions for making a banjo out of an old cigar box, or a field telephone with bladders from the butcher. With its help I made, over and over, lath and brown paper kites of many shapes that flew beautifully, and elastic-driven model aeroplanes that flew badly, if at all. With no need for any guidance but trial and error I made bows from stout branches of yew or ash, and arrows from laths; catapults at first from garter elastic, but then with strong, square-sectioned elastic from the ironmonger (who could also be persuaded to sell us half a pound of gunpowder for home-made cannon and miniature landmines). A row of bottles on the garden wall made a first-rate target for catapult and sling, and for the Daisy and King airguns that succeeded them.

'From then on the whole countryside was my playground. My family were country builders, and beyond the garden wall was a paddock for Peter and Betsy, our two ponies, and at its far end a rambling complex of sheds and stables with lofts to hide in and roofs to climb. In the paddock, with the great wooden packing cases in which slabs of stone had come, I and my friends would build huts and forts, and turn and turn about besiege and defend them against slings, stones, and arrows, not without casualties.

'And quarter of a mile away my friend Bernard lived. His father's dairy farm had rambling buildings and orchards where we used to play a daylong game of prisoner's base which we called, I cannot tell why, I-Urky. Right through its fields there ran the ''beck'', the river Rase from which Market Rasen takes its name: a shallow, sandy stream, not too wide for leaping, running between high banks. There we would fish for ''stonies''—that is, loach—and sticklebacks, and tickle small trout under the overhanging banks, and dam the stream with sods cut from its own margins until it piled up four feet deep, so that we could make ''one long bathing of a summer's day'', and then release a thrilling rush of waters. Or, another time, we would dig out a wasp's nest—a perilous business— to take the grubs as bait, and go fishing in the deep ''brickpits'', the abandoned workings of the local brickworks. Then when work had finished for the day we would slip the little iron clay trucks from their endless chain and ride wildly downhill on them. And further afield still there was ''the warren'', a great sandy common ringed with woods, where I used to chase butterflies, and look for adders as they lay in the heather, basking in the spring sunshine.

'And after that came the age of bats, and balls and tennis racquets, but that is another story.'

How idyllic, given even modest circumstances, Edwardian childhoods seem to be! Toys and dolls are cherished in the memory as part of the fabric of childhood; and for grandmama and grandpapa the memories of their remoter past are, of course, the greenest. Mavis Strange's and John Scupham's childhoods were English to the core, but many of the toys they played with would not be English in origin: some, from their descriptions, are identifiably German. England had, however, by the early years of the century, its own craftsmen and inventors of distinction, both in constructional toys and in dollmaking.

Dollmakers I

England never rivalled France or Germany in the production of bisque dolls; but in two kindred fields her reputation was now supreme. The tradition of wax doll making, established by craftsmen of Italian origin—Montanari, Pierotti— was being sustained with equal distinction by others of native stock, such as Lucy Peck; while Dean's rag dolls were bringing to the mass market a new concept: the doll as a plaything for the very young—cuddly, infinitely pliable, and made for affection; yet often jokey too, and well able to survive the roughest punishment.

Lucy Peck, recalled by her granddaughter

'My "Granny" Lucy Peck, née Brightman, born in 1846 and married to Henry Peck in 1876, had retired from business before I knew her. From 1894 to 1908, during the years of my Granny's prime as an internationally known wax doll maker and repairer, my mother Ethel Frances Lucy and my uncle Howard were growing up, and the family lived over my granny's shop, at 151 Regent Street.

'At this time her husband, who had qualified as a pharmacist, ran a chemist's shop elsewhere. He was little interested in business management and spent much time reading philosophy and Shakespeare. In later years he acted Shakespearean parts, and indeed played opposite Margaret Rutherford before she turned professional.

'Lucy Peck died in 1930. She and her husband had moved to Kingston-on-Thames in 1922. On retirement she gave up modelling in wax to learn to model in clay (at the age of seventy-six) at Kingston College of Art; and my grandfather then made up a prescription for her as to "how to cast in Plaster of Paris".

'But for me she will always be the mother of my mother, and the frail little woman whose hair had once been Irish red but was always white for me. I can see now her delicate hands showing me the intricate brass cogs in the mechanism of a giant Victorian musical box on which she played tunes to me while she rested on her chaise longue.

'I had gifts of toys (which I still possess) kept back for me after the closure of the business: a doll's house and furniture including a miniature oil painting and a double pewter candlestick and a fair-haired china doll with closing eyes. Wax dolls were too fragile for play purposes.

'And I still remember the special occasion when my grandmother was the first to inscribe her name "Lucy Peck" against her birth date of 22nd March in my new Kate Greenaway's *Birthday Book for Children*.

Facing: Miniature replicas of a peeress's robes worn at King Edward VII's coronation. They were made by 'Fat Jane', the devoted nanny of the peeress's daughter, *Pollock's Toy Museum*

Inset: Wax doll by Lucy Peck, representing Queen Victoria, in her nightdress, on the morning she became queen

Below: Lucy Peck: her style of doll, her sampler, and her portrait

Edwardian wax doll with
contemporary games and Louis
Wain cat book

Charles Pierotti, remembered by his niece

'My great-great-grandfather, Domenico Pierotti, came to England as a boy in 1770, to receive medical treatment after falling out of a tree. He stayed in Portsmouth with his mother's sister, who made a variety of things involving modelling and moulding: wall and ceiling panels coated with plaster, milliners' figures of papier maché coated with wax, and dolls made in the same way. Domenico learned many of the skills of his uncle and aunt, and eventually established himself in London. It was his ninth child, Anericho Cephas (known as Henry or Harry), who specialised in making wax dolls of prominent persons by the poured wax method. He showed his dolls in exhibitions, including the Great Exhibition of 1851, and won medals for them. His shop was at 108 Oxford Street.

'Anericho's family of twelve also included a dollmaker, my grandfather Charles William. He carried on the business from 43 Crawford Street. He was also involved in display work, making hairdressers' models for wigs, and tailors' models; and he made and repaired dolls for Queen Victoria. It seems probable that my grandfather used many of the original moulds, for the type of doll head with Pierotti features remained consistent over a long period.

'When, in 1892, he died of lead poisoning—one of the then occupational risks of this industry—his widow continued making wax dolls until she was ninety, with the help of her two sons, Harry and Charles Ernest, and three of her daughters, one of whom is now in her 93rd year. The dolls were marketed in various shops in the West End of London, especially at Hamley's, Regent Street.

'I can remember as a child, whenever we came to town, being taken to see Uncle Charles's dolls, extravagantly dressed and standing in the window awaiting their fortunate and wealthy little buyers. They were taken up to Hamley's by Hansom cab, and the small ones were sold to them for 2s 6d.

'I well remember, too, my grandmother's house at 324 Goldhawk Road, Shepherds' Bush, where many members of her large family and their husbands, wives and children would gather at week-ends. I especially remember the wonderful cakes she used to make for us children, such as I have never tasted since.

'Most fascinating of all, in the large old kitchen downstairs at the back, used as a workroom, I remember my uncles at work. They were dear, kindly men, painstaking in their work, somewhat unbusinesslike, and quite patient with the little girl who dodged in unobserved, she hoped, to see what was going on, and became absorbed in the details of the huge cauldrons warming up on the old kitchen range (the smell of wax pervaded the house, and lingers in my nostrils even now); and the irregular shapes of plaster moulds lined along the shelves or benches, ready for the next batch of heads or limbs; and the boxes and boxes of eyes—all too soon to be chased out by aunt or parent saying "Uncle does not want to be disturbed".

'I remember too the view from the window of the garden with the magnificent pear tree, so heavily laden with fruit in which we all shared each year for many

Wax-over-papier maché composition dolls' heads

55

years. And I can see now my aunts and our mother busily cutting up calico for the bodies of dolls and machining the pieces together. To complete a doll, wax heads and limbs were sewn on to a stuffed fabric body.

'My grandmother was ninety-two when she died in the 1930s, and I suppose the fashion for wax dolls was dying out. Even those I wheeled out in a pram were thought to be curiosities by other children, and I'm sure the practical china ones were more popular. I was never allowed to play with my wax dolls, or dress and undress them, or put them near the fire in case they melted; so I would say they were not a success with children.

'It was not until I was quite grown up that I realised how fortunate I was in possessing six of the Pierotti dolls, carefully treasured by my mother who was of course well aware of their value. All my dolls were dressed by my mother in clothes of the period most beautifully made by hand, with tuck lace insertions and bows which are still in good condition to-day. In my collection I have two of the baby dolls, a fairy doll, a child doll and an Italian doll—the only one of its kind in existence, and one of the last ever made by my Uncle Charles, as a fortune teller for a bazaar, before his retirement. It is sad that he should have spent his life making dolls for children, as his own only child, a boy, died at birth.

'I still have a vivid picture of my Uncle Charlie, busy in his workroom with his

Dean's Rag Book Co
advertisement, 1913 in
The Toy Trader

Right: Dean's Rag Doll with skin-covered horse,
Pollock's Toy Museum

56

spectacles thrust well up over his forehead as he worked on the faces of the dolls with his modelling tools. Every doll was finished by hand.

'Of the present generation, my cousins, it is sad that no one has carried on the tradition of wax doll making. I would have liked to try, but the thought of a woman taking on a trade was not viewed very hopefully in those days. However, members of the next generation may yet prove to have made their mark in the artistic world, who knows?'

Dean's Rag Dolls

The printing and publishing firm of Dean & Son had been established in the City of London since the 18th century, first in Threadneedle Street and later on Ludgate Hill, near the centre of the printing trade. Dean's were among the first to produce children's books designed for entertainment as much as for instruction: pictorial alphabets, for instance, or Perrault's fairy tales with liberal illustration and a minimum of text. From the 1840s onwards they produced all kinds of ingenious movable-flap and three-dimensional books, strung together with ribbons: a typical example was *Dissolving Pictures of Things Worth Knowing*, published in 1862.

Colouring by hand with stencils gave way around 1870 to oil colour printing; and soon afterwards the experiment was made of pasting the printed pages on to calico to strengthen them (as is done with maps). In 1901 this process was superseded in turn by direct printing to 'holland' calico. The rag book had arrived.

'Dean's first rag book title was *The Life of Bold AB on his Ship in the Rolling C*. The colours were fast, the product certified as hygenic. The pages could be washed without damage, and sucked with impunity: perfect, in fact for children who in the words of the rag book's originator, 'wear their food and eat their clothes'. The book was an immediate success.

So in 1905 a subsidiary firm, Dean's Rag Book Company, was formed, to specialise in rag books and, very soon, rag dolls also. First of these was the Big Baby Doll, thirty inches high, and designed to be dressed in cast-off baby clothes. It was printed in colour on calico, like the books, and sold flat in the sheet, to be cut and sewn at home, for 1s 6d. The rag doll quickly became popular, but many customers disliked the trouble of cutting, sewing and stuffing; so Dean's devised machinery for doing this, and sold the dolls ready-made also.

From relatively crude beginnings, a succession of developments over the next decade, always in the direction of greater realism, brought considerable technical sophistication to the rag doll. In 1913 Dean's patented the "Tru-to-Life" face, in which a pressed moulded mask behind the doll's face gave its features a three-dimensional quality. Later, the same method was applied to animal dolls; while another patent was taken out for the 'Evripoze' body which could maintain its head and limbs posed in any attitude, naturalistic or caricatured, without the aid of ball-and-socket joints or springs.

From 1914 on, Dean's Rag Book Company turned out a profusion of character dolls: Betty Blue, the goggle-eyed Moppietops, Carrie Cuddler, Shrieking Susan, Piccadilly Nut—to name but a few. The outbreak of war spawned a shoal of patriotic toys: soldiers and sailors with Union Jacks, John Bull, and—more originally—Tommy Fuzbuz, a soft busbied set of soldier ninepins with ball, together with a book *All about Tommy Fuzbuz*. After the war, topicality was captured in other ways: the Music Hall hit of 1921, 'Gilbert the Filbert, the Nursery Knut', quickly earned his rag doll counterpart.

By the 1920s other materials, particularly felt and plush, were being used for dollmaking; and alongside the printed rag dolls there were Cosy Kid dolls in bonnets, berets and gaiters, and Jumper dolls in 'fashionable attire and Tam o' Shanters'. Animals, too—some printed, some in 'fluffidown'—were enlisted in their dozens into the ranks of Dean's soft toys; and some (like the Scootazoo bear on wheels, snappily dressed in stripy trousers, check jacket and spotted scarf) wryly reflected in caricature the foibles of their human creators.

Pierotti wax doll, 1919,
Worthing Museum

57

An old-style Midland "Single-wheeler"

American 4-4-2 Locomotive

A typical Meccano Tank Loco.

Electric Freight Loco.

The new Meccano

The career of Frank Hornby, inventor of Meccano, reads like a tract celebrating the Victorian virtues— self-help, persistence, and success. Born in 1863 the son of a Liverpool provision merchant, he worked humbly enough until past forty, first in his father's, then in another importing firm. From his father he had inherited a dogged toughness; from his mother a more dreamy, visionary quality. He was inclined to truant from school, but in order to read and learn more, not less. As a young man he sang enthusiastically and organised concert parties in the Band of Hope, a temperance society. But his paradise was his workshop, where he was for ever tinkering with metal.

Married, Hornby delighted in inventing and making toys for his children. But there was a continual demand for new ones, and for each new toy new parts had to be made. He needed parts that could be applied in different ways to different models, and some standard way of fitting part to part; and gradually the idea came to him of parts all perforated with a series of holes the same size and the same distance apart. Such parts could, he realised, be bolted up to a model in different positions and at different angles; and having done their work in one model could be unbolted and applied to another.

Hornby found next to nothing ready to hand. He had to make all his nuts and bolts himself. He had to design his own wheels, have them cast in a local foundry and turned on the lathe. 'It was a great day for me and my boys', he recalled thirty years later, 'when I built up my first meccano crane, which ran on wheels and luffed and jibbed splendidly, just like a real crane. What delight we had in taking the crane to pieces and building it up again! Before we attached the jib, the base of the crane looked so much like a truck that we added a few more strips and made it into a real truck.'

Hornby's concept of interchangeable parts had proved itself. So had his claim that Meccano (originally marketed as Mechanics Made Easy) illustrated basic engineering principles—a claim fully endorsed by Professor Hele-Shaw of University College, Liverpool, to whom Hornby had submitted details of his models.

Hornby patented his invention in 1901; but to launch Meccano effectively he had to turn manufacturer himself. More years of toil and moil followed in his first primitive, one-room factory. But it was not drudgery. 'I and my chief assistant', he relates, 'used to stay behind in our one-roomed factory after the others had gone home and bring out the acid vats and dip the wheels. We had no proper system of ventilation, so that the fumes from the acid nearly choked us. When matters got too bad we had to suspend operations abruptly, and dash out into the open air to recover.'

From this little factory in Duke Street, Liverpool, Meccano later moved to larger premises at West Derby Road, and finally to a brand-new, purpose-built factory at Old Swan, on the city's outskirts. From then on there was no holding it. Meccano invaded the world, sired the Meccano Guild—an international fraternity of Meccano fans—and the Meccano Magazine. Hornby trains followed in the wake of Meccano, and by 1925 Frank Hornby's air of confident authority—the domed forehead, the piercing eyes, the waxed moustaches— proclaimed the successful business tycoon. This role, too, he relished; but kept also to the end his boy-scout enthusiasm and his genuine sense of educational purpose. Three quarters of a century after its first patent Meccano lives and thrives still—as solid and muscular, amid its flabbier imitators, as the Forth Rail Bridge.

From *Meccano Magazine* 1927

Toy shops

From Gamage's catalogue, 1913

Below: English Wax Doll, and
Dolly Dimple,
a paper dressing doll

'Hamley's, England'. Seventy-five years ago, as to-day, this was a sufficient address for letters to reach London's largest and best-known toyshop. At that time, however, it still stood at 86 High Holborn, on the site of the original 'Noah's Ark' toyshop which had been started by Mr William Henry Hamley's forefathers in 1760. William Henry himself, born in 1843, established the world-wide reputation of the shop by building up an ever-expanding wholesale business alongside his retail trading. His personal interest in conjuring made the shop a depot for magicians and stage conjurers, who found there new and ingenious novelties; for he realised there was a profitable market in practical jokes and parlour tricks. It was a time when exploding cigars, rubber roses for the lapel that squirted water, boxes of sneezing powder, and telescopes that left black eyes were all the rage. But in 1900 Hamley's was known, above all, as the firm that had launched the great craze for a new game: Ping Pong.

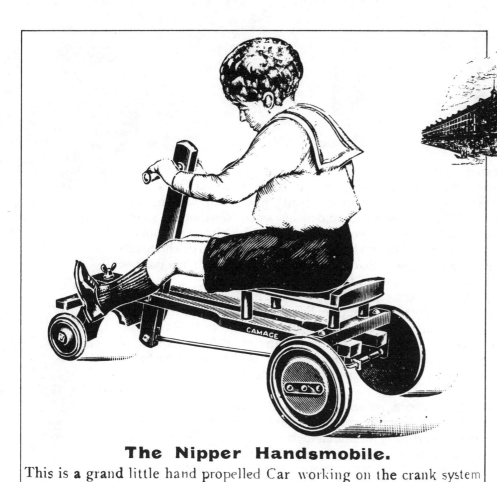

The Nipper Handsmobile.

This is **a** grand little hand propelled Car working on the crank system
Strong and perfectly safe.   Splendid value.   Price **8 9**

Gamage's shop in 1904, illustrated in *The Daily Mail*

Left: The Nipper Handsmobile, from Gamage's catalogue 1913

Below: Mr William Henry Hamley. His obituary notice in *Games and Toys*, August 1916, recorded that 'The late Mr Hamley was a very smart man, and was never seen without a silk hat, beautifully polished, and a flower in his buttonhole.'

Overleaf: Street Hawkers on Ludgate Hill at Christmastide, 1906—from *The Graphic*

HAMLEY'S CABINET OF MAGIC.

No. 7 CABINET. Price 3 Guineas.

No. 1.—Box of Magic, contains Six Tricks, of superior finish, with full directions. *Price* 2/6. *Post free* 2/9.

No. 2.—P___ ___ins Ten Wonderful Tricks, with___ ___ *Post free* 6/-.

No. 3.—E___ ___or Tricks of a ___ ___us. *Post free* 11___

No. 4.— ___ ___6/-.

No. 5.— ___ ___2/-.

No. 6.— ___ ___. A handsom___ ___ment of s___ ___hing's entertain___ ___ction from the ___ ___V. and F. Ham___ ___ending this as___ ___mateur conjuro___ ___reatest satisfac___ ___perfec-tion of ___ ___which the mo___ ___ed, with full print___ ___paid on *receipt*.

Also an assortment of startling illusions, adapted for amateurs, in boxes, with printed instructions, at 3, 4, 5, *and* 10 Guineas *per box*.

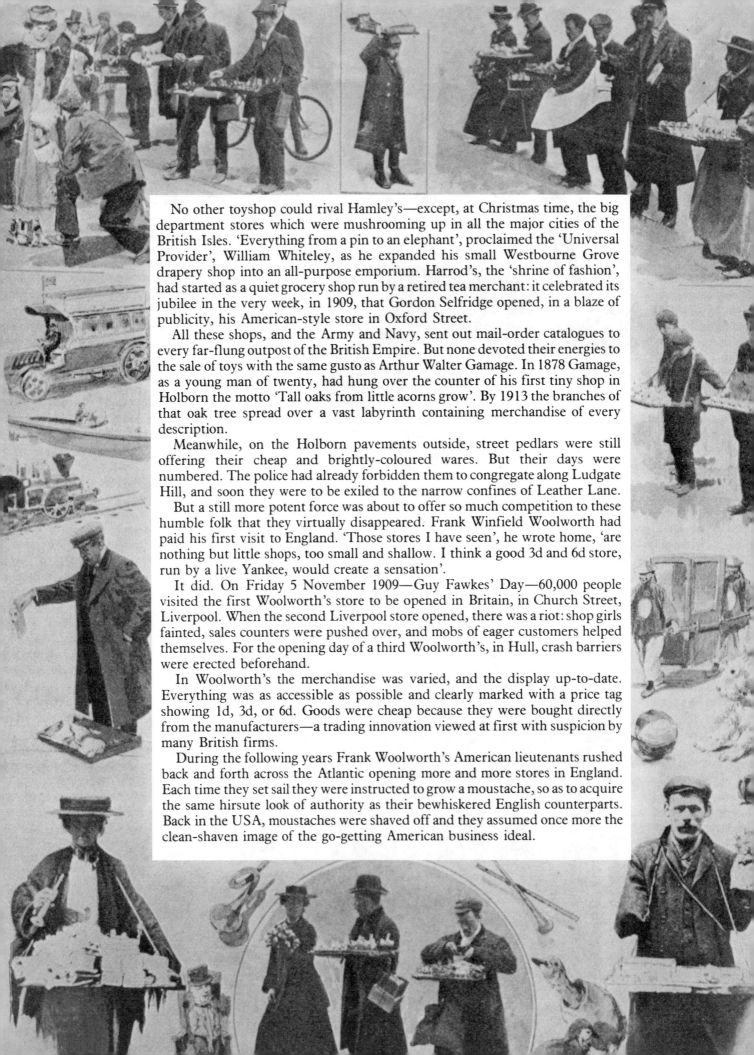

No other toyshop could rival Hamley's—except, at Christmas time, the big department stores which were mushrooming up in all the major cities of the British Isles. 'Everything from a pin to an elephant', proclaimed the 'Universal Provider', William Whiteley, as he expanded his small Westbourne Grove drapery shop into an all-purpose emporium. Harrod's, the 'shrine of fashion', had started as a quiet grocery shop run by a retired tea merchant: it celebrated its jubilee in the very week, in 1909, that Gordon Selfridge opened, in a blaze of publicity, his American-style store in Oxford Street.

All these shops, and the Army and Navy, sent out mail-order catalogues to every far-flung outpost of the British Empire. But none devoted their energies to the sale of toys with the same gusto as Arthur Walter Gamage. In 1878 Gamage, as a young man of twenty, had hung over the counter of his first tiny shop in Holborn the motto 'Tall oaks from little acorns grow'. By 1913 the branches of that oak tree spread over a vast labyrinth containing merchandise of every description.

Meanwhile, on the Holborn pavements outside, street pedlars were still offering their cheap and brightly-coloured wares. But their days were numbered. The police had already forbidden them to congregate along Ludgate Hill, and soon they were to be exiled to the narrow confines of Leather Lane.

But a still more potent force was about to offer so much competition to these humble folk that they virtually disappeared. Frank Winfield Woolworth had paid his first visit to England. 'Those stores I have seen', he wrote home, 'are nothing but little shops, too small and shallow. I think a good 3d and 6d store, run by a live Yankee, would create a sensation'.

It did. On Friday 5 November 1909—Guy Fawkes' Day—60,000 people visited the first Woolworth's store to be opened in Britain, in Church Street, Liverpool. When the second Liverpool store opened, there was a riot: shop girls fainted, sales counters were pushed over, and mobs of eager customers helped themselves. For the opening day of a third Woolworth's, in Hull, crash barriers were erected beforehand.

In Woolworth's the merchandise was varied, and the display up-to-date. Everything was as accessible as possible and clearly marked with a price tag showing 1d, 3d, or 6d. Goods were cheap because they were bought directly from the manufacturers—a trading innovation viewed at first with suspicion by many British firms.

During the following years Frank Woolworth's American lieutenants rushed back and forth across the Atlantic opening more and more stores in England. Each time they set sail they were instructed to grow a moustache, so as to acquire the same hirsute look of authority as their bewhiskered English counterparts. Back in the USA, moustaches were shaved off and they assumed once more the clean-shaven image of the go-getting American business ideal.

The toy trade

For the year 1913 Gamage's catalogue devoted nearly 300 pages to toys, games, books, puzzles and sports equipment which could be mail ordered or bought in 'The People's Emporium'. Of these only the larger items such as rocking horses, prams and pedal cars—all difficult to transport—were made in England. Nearly all the other items were imported, mostly from Germany. German export figures for 1915 show that 64,000 tons of toys were exported that year, valued at £5,000,000; and that of this amount more than two-thirds went to Great Britain and the USA. Virtually the entire toy trade in England was dominated by German firms.

Five years before this, in 1908, an enterprising journalist, Mr W B Tattersall, had launched *The Toy Trader* Ten years later, in the September issue of *The Toy and Fancy Goods Trader*, as it had then become, he recalls his early struggles:

'The life-blood of a trade journal is, of course, advertising. Without its advertisers no journal of this type can succeed. But when I set out to get support of this nature I discovered what a close corporation the toy trade really was. The Germans had captured the trade, and the Germans meant to keep the trade.

'It was heart-breaking trying to get through this German ring. The leaders of it jeered at me; and even many purely British firms treated my venture in the same way because they were so much in the power of the German houses that they would not or could not go contrary to their wishes. Up to the outbreak of hostilities—with a few very notable exceptions—it seemed impossible to develop the toy industry in this country. If a new man started making toys his output was promptly absorbed by the German octopus, who took care to see that the manufacturer made very little money out of his enterprise.'

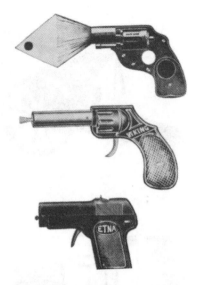

The Hun Gun (top of the three pistols) cost 3d, including three extra exploders. 'If the simple directions are followed', said the advertisement, 'a small child can produce a tremendous report'.

Left: Fort, English, First World War period

Mr R Simmonds, founder of *Games and Toys*, a second trade journal, which started publication in June 1914

From top: The New Model
Mountain Gun, by Oliver, Harper
and Co, 1917;
The Whitanco Laundelette, made
by Whiteley Tansley, 1919;
eight-inch mechanical tank,
Whiteley Tansley, 1919;
Destroyer, by Oliver, Harper and
Co, 1917

Facing: Ships by Meccano;
Joey aeroplane by R Joseph and
Co; Fretwork ambulance
probably by Hobbies Ltd; Field-
Gun & Tank by Lord Roberts
Memorial Workshops Ltd

The low price of German toys was based on the use of badly-paid outworkers. Conditions in England had until recently been no better. Mr HS Jarvis, director of the firm Patterson Edwards, which made large wooden toys, gave this account in 1919 of his early days in the trade:

'It is some thirty-three years since I commenced to manufacture wood toys, and this beginning was as primitive as it could be. In those days Houndsditch was the famous centre for the accumulation of London-made toys. On any Friday afternoon or Saturday morning down the 'Ditch' from Bishopsgate, for a distance of some fifty yards, would extend a row of barrows, each with its modest load (probably a week's output) of toys. These were busily unloaded, often by the maker himself assisted by a boy (no girls then), and the goods delivered into the adjoining warehouses. Cash on delivery were the terms, and the week's wage of many a factory depended on this prompt payment.

'To-day, the "Ditch" is empty. In place of the 40s or 60s worth of toys on each of twenty barrows, making a big show of little, round the corners in back streets vans with huge consignments will unload. A larger, cleaner and healthier trade is about to begin—merchandise produced not in hovels, but in decent factories, with the workman better off than his employer of thirty years ago . . .

'For some ten years my efforts in the toy industry resulted in slow progress. Then I managed to purchase my first wood-working machine: it was a hand-power saw-bench, turned with a wheel. I got a strong, willing lad to turn the wheel; we earned 2s 6d an hour at it, and it was the Wheel of Fortune. In some four months, the extra revenue from this enabled me to take larger premises and purchase the nucleus of a power plant. The struggle to support this was more than I care to remember. The purchase was made in a January and eight months of no trade faced me. Our nightmare was that the money we made in the autumn we lost in the spring.'

The outbreak of war in 1914 put an immediate stop to German imports, and during the war years a new industry, fostered by the government, was gradually established in Britain. By the end of hostilities the toy trade was employing more than 100,000 workers, including many thousands of discharged and disabled soldiers and sailors.

The first toys were sometimes rather crude and badly finished. Yet it was during those difficult years that many firms still in existence fifty years later gained the experience and knowledge which were the foundation of their future success. Mr John Hamley, son of W H Hamley, writing to *The Toy and Fancy Goods Trader* in September 1918, looked forward to a bright future for the trade given certain conditions:

'During the six years immediately preceding the war, a steady flow of German and Austrian goods came to this country at prices with which we could not compete: this made the development of the home industry slow, in goods mechanical more especially. On the outbreak of war dealers were forced to find entirely new sources of supply, and a moment of great opportunity came for the existing English manufacturers, who in circumstances of the greatest difficulty, with labour and materials woefully short, have done marvellously well. I foresee a great future for the trade, if only a substantial tariff is built up against imported goods.

'At present we do not pay sufficient attention to the finish of our goods, and have not grasped the importance of appearance, good boxing and so on, but doubtless this will come with time and experience. We will happily never be able to compete with German sweated and child labour, so a tariff is vital.'

The tariff Hamley demanded was not forthcoming, and the immediate post-war years were fraught with difficulties. But this is to anticipate: first, let us look more closely at the dollmakers at work during the war.

From the magazine *Fretwork*, published by Hobbies Ltd. The 'tank to make yourself' (April 1917) is described as 'passed by the censor'

Below: Glydos Scooters, 1915

Dollmakers II

A pioneer factory in the Potteries

At the outbreak of war in 1914 the firm of S Hancock & Sons, Wolfe Street, Stoke-on-Trent, began making little china ornaments with Allied flags and other patriotic devices for the fancy goods trade. Soon after, they were commissioned to produce the Fumsup china mascot doll for Hamley's. From this, it was only a step to embarking on the regular production of dolls' heads—a complex and highly specialised technique which required a lot of preliminary research and experiment.

An article in *Games and Toys* for August 1917 describes a visit to Hancock's pottery and the processes of making dolls' heads there. First, the china clay is ground and mixed with other materials and with water until it is in a fluid state, known as 'slip'. The slip is then taken to the casting shops, where vast numbers of plaster of Paris moulds await it. The preparation of these moulds has involved dozens of designs, and modellers working from them like so many sculptors.

In the casting shop, the article goes on to explain, 'the two parts of the mould are put together and the slip is poured in until the mould is quite full. As we watch it, we see the slip very slowly receding down the aperture or orifice; and Mr Hancock explains to us that the mould is drawing away by capillary attraction the water from the slip, and that a film of the china clay is forming on the mould. This process goes on so rapidly that in about five minutes the film is sufficiently thick to enable the mould to be turned upside down and the remaining slip poured away. In a very short time the mould can be opened, and in it will be found the china head, which is placed after one day in an adjacent drying stove.'

Next, the eyes are cut out—a delicate process, as the apertures must be absolutely correct, and must be carefully bevelled inside the head to allow the eyes to be inserted later. Inequalities in the surface of the head are now removed by means of a heavy camel hair brush dipped in water; and after drying, the head is now ready for the ovens, to which it passes by way of the 'green house', a huge room kept at constant temperature.

'Mr Hancock', the report goes on, 'permitted us to enter one of these great ovens (called a bisque oven) when it was being prepared for firing. It reminded one somewhat of a big crypt. It is built in circular form, of brick, and is some fifteen feet across, gradually sloping up to a pointed dome about twenty feet high. It is heated by means of external fires built in its walls: these, kept going day and night, soon produce in it a heat of about 1,200 C.

'We are next taken to see the heads being packed ready to go in the oven. They are placed in large earthenware pans made of marl and having a practically flat bottom. These pans or "saggars" are taken one by one to the oven, where the first are placed on the ground next to the wall until a ring of them is formed round it. Others are brought in and stood on top of the first ring until that in turn is completed; then others are built on these until they form a complete lining. Next, the door is closed, and the fires are made up and kept going night and day until finally they are drawn, the oven opened and the saggars removed.

'Damaged heads are now discarded, and the remainder pass to the decorators. The lips are painted in by hand, also the eyelashes, and little touches are given to the nostrils. Sometimes the complexion too is hand-painted; sometimes it is entrusted to aerograph operators. Then the decorating work has to be baked in; so the head must go again to what is known as the enamelling kiln, which makes the colouring permanent.

'Finally', concludes the report, 'we were able to see the eyes being inserted. If they are fixed eyes it is quite a simple process: they need only to be very accurately placed in position and held there by a plaster of Paris backing. But in the case of sleeping eyes a much more elaborate operation is necessary.

'We were a little disappointed that we were unable to see the process of glass eye making, which is known to be carried on at Messrs. Hancock's works.

68

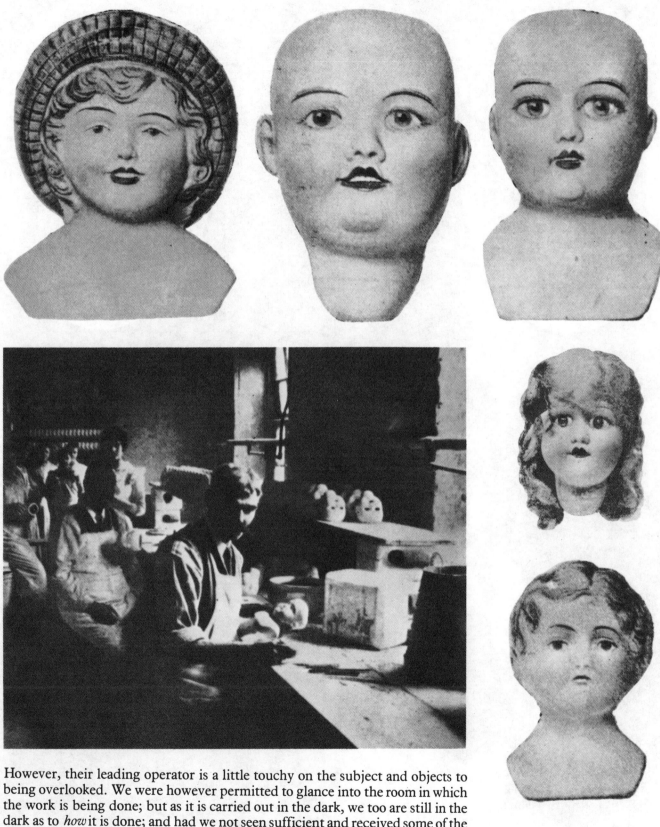

However, their leading operator is a little touchy on the subject and objects to being overlooked. We were however permitted to glance into the room in which the work is being done; but as it is carried out in the dark, we too are still in the dark as to *how* it is done; and had we not seen sufficient and received some of the glass eyes (much too hot to hold) we should have been sceptical as to what process was going on. We are confident that this department will in the future make the firm independent of either France or Germany for the production of glass eyes necessary to meet their requirements.'

Thwarted by industrial security, the visiting party nevertheless speaks up for Britain!

Dolls heads advertised by Hancock & Sons

69

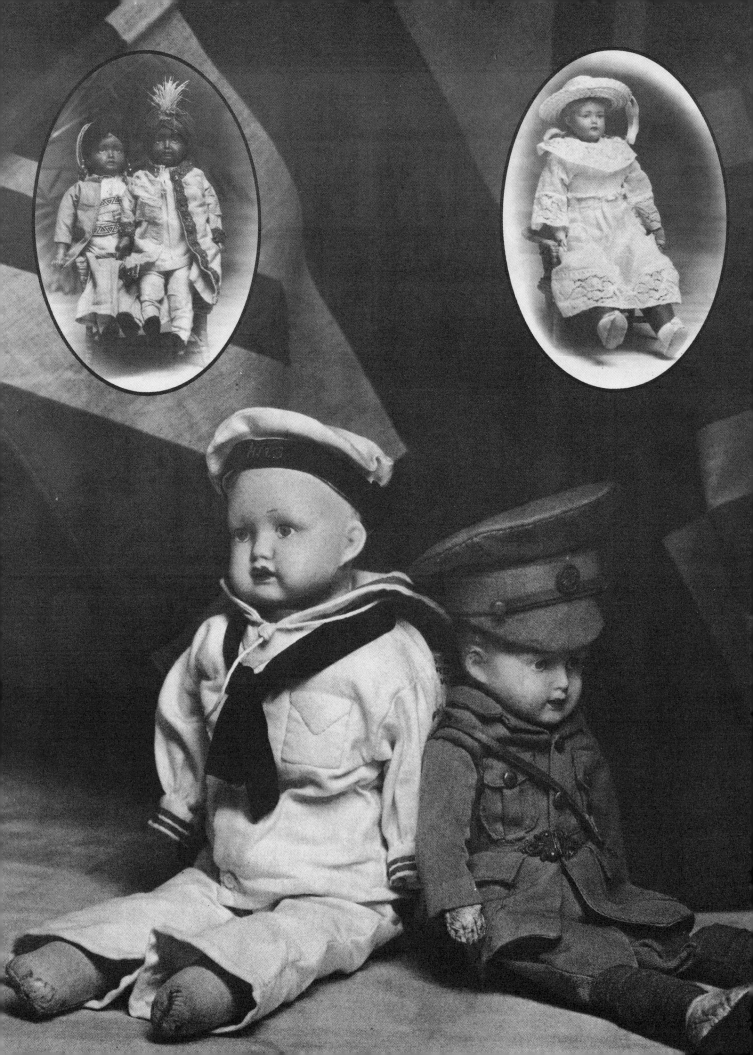

From china to composition dolls

Hancock and Sons were not the only large, well-established pottery to turn their hand during the war years to making dolls' heads and limbs. Many of the firms which in addition to their ordinary run of table-ware were producing china novelties and sea-side holiday souvenirs found that, after a period of trial and error, they could manufacture passable china heads. Thus WH Goss, specialists in heraldic crested china, made dolls' heads for the Potteries Toy Company, set up by Mrs Rittner, wife of the local MP, at Stoke-on-Trent to help mitigate the distress caused by the upheavals of war. Hewitt and Leadbeater of Longton made heads marked 'Willow', while continuing their formidable output of Ann Hathaway cottages and other mementoes. Mayer and Sheratt, at the Clifton works, made dolls marked 'Melba'.

Smaller firms also came into existence—like the Dura Porcelain Co, founded at Elm Street, Hanley, in 1915, by two working potters and a colour expert. And a great variety of workshops sprang up for the finishing jobs: attaching the heads and limbs on to stuffed rag bodies, and dressing the completed dolls.

Some of these new firms were quite small affairs: a few women stitching and sewing in a back parlour. Others, like Toyland, set up by Mr George Henry Buckmaster, manager of the Shelton branch of the newsagents WH Smith and

Sons, grew into very large concerns making a wide variety of toys. Others again, like W Speight Ltd of Dewsbury in the West Riding, concentrated their efforts on dolls alone, placing huge orders in the Potteries for dolls' heads marked with their own brand name 'Classic'.

At Mirfield, a few miles out of Dewsbury on the main Huddersfield road, there still stands to-day a solid brick building bearing over its main entrance, in bold 1920 lettering, the words 'Classic Works'. Inside, from the darkened hallway one is shown into a long room, where suddenly a myriad of lights are switched on, and one is surrounded by lampshades in every conceivable colour, shape and material. 'It was in my father's time,' explains Mr AK Speight, 'that the firm moved out of the centre of Dewsbury and went over to making lampshades. The doll business was really my grandfather's creation. He started life as a hairdresser, and specialised in making hair pieces and theatrical wigs. He had large works in Dewsbury where they made the wire frames and pads used for the elaborate hair-dos of those days. He sold crepe hair, mohair, and doll hair to other manufacturers, and exported a lot to Germany and other places. I don't really know much about the doll making, as I was born after my grandfather died; and when I came into the business my father had completely switched to lampshades. I think we must have made the last lot of dolls at Speight's round about 1928. I do know that my grandfather ran a dolls' hospital and did repairs as well as making dolls.'

The pages of the *Toy Trader* for August 1917, in an article entitled 'A Great Doll Factory', give many more details. They tell how, at the outbreak of war, The Board of Trade approached Messrs Speight and asked them if they could make dolls' wigs. After a dolls' wig department had been established, they were asked to take up making dolls' bodies also; and by 1917 the sample range in their London showrooms consisted of over 1,000 designs, while their large, up-to-date factory in Dewsbury employed over 500 workers in stuffing the dolls' bodies, fixing the china dolls' heads and limbs, and making wigs, shoes, hats, dresses and finally boxes to pack the finished dolls in. Speight's 1920 catalogue advertises: Dinkee dolls in five sizes with sleeping eyes, real mohair wigs, best china heads, composition arms and legs, clothes made to take off with hooks and eyes, shoes, socks, hat and muff—nicely boxed and priced from 5s 4d to 22s 6d; Kidette Classic Dolls, fully jointed by the latest process, with hair-stuffed bodies, best English china heads, veined glass eyes, and five different styles of wig—from 18s 6d; Classic Baby Doll, plus a range of dolls such as Dazzle Dazzle, Georgette, Red Riding Hood, Miss Muffet, Flossy, and Sailor, Seaside, Pyjama or Dutch girls which really only differ according to the style of dress and the materials used.

Dolls' Hair

in various qualities and styles of make-up—
Straight, Wavy, Ringlet and Creped.

Top: Speight's Ltd Classic Works, Dewsbury

Facing page: Classic dolls, Dinkie, 1919, Cecily, Dazzle Dazzle, and design 1003 A/D
Pollock's Toy Museum

The dolls' heads and limbs produced in the Potteries in the First World War were for the most part attached to bodies made from cheapish cotton, imitation 'kid' leather, or a rather poor quality shiny material akin to thin oilcloth. These stuffed bodies were by far the easiest to manufacture as they could be quickly made up on a sewing machine. To-day, however, English dolls' heads are often found attached to bodies moulded out of various compositions of wood pulp and sawdust and different glues. A close inspection of these dolls reveals that they have at some time in their fifty years of life been to a dolls' hospital, and that the English head is a replacement, fixed to a body originally made in France or Germany. Pollock's Toy Museum has several such hybrid dolls: a Classic head on a Jumeau composition body, for instance, and a Melba head on a very much older hand-stitched leather body.

However, some composition bodies were made in England. In their issue of October 1913 *The Toy and Fancy Goods Trader* reported the existence, at 89 Milton Street, London EC, of a firm Messrs Kean and Co, manufacturing a new and very strong composition body for china heads imported from Germany. Subsequently, when the Trading with the Enemy Act came to be rigorously applied, it was revealed that J Kohnstam, Kean and Co was only a front for a German firm. The Vera dolls they made did not, however, disappear; for very soon afterwards we find the name again in large advertisements for the toys made by disabled soldiers and sailors at Lord Roberts's Memorial Workshops in the Fulham Road, London,—but with the china heads replaced by composition ones. A reporter from *The Toy and Fancy Goods Trader*, visiting the factory in February 1918, describes the production of 'the exquisite Vera doll in its seven sizes, ranging from 15½ inches to 27 inches, as well as a range of character baby dolls and a number of those cunning little Kewpies so dear to the novelty-loving public.

'These are all made from a secret composition which is practically unbreakable, the moulds being filled by a process which is protected by a patent. Every jointed doll, even the smallest, has twenty separate parts, and in addition to the moulders, a number of men are employed in turning and shaping the various wooden parts and ball sockets which go to make up the body of the doll. In this section there are at least a dozen different machines used, such as the pendulum saw, rounding machine, drilling machine, automatic lathe, etc, etc, each of which is suitable for the use of a one-armed man.'

To overcome wartime shortages many experiments were made. Some manufacturers, like Nunn and Smeed of Liverpool, prided themselves on a new secret finish which did away with paint, and resembled porcelain. Moreover, it was both non-poisonous and waterproof. The Dolls' Accessory Company of Longton, Staffs went one step further. In addition to their Ise all Dicky and other china figures they put on the market a series of Flesho dolls' heads. These dolls had china heads coated with a film of wax to improve their rather inferior complexions.

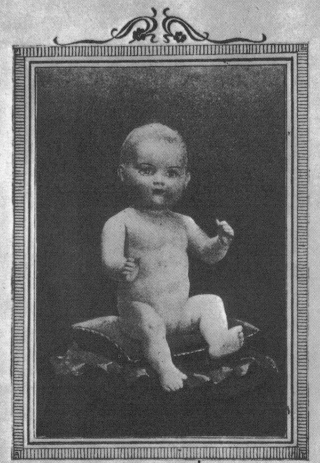
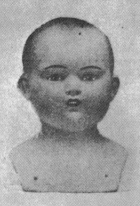

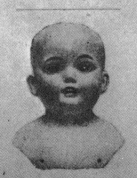

From an advertisement by Hewitt & Leadbeater, Stoke-on-Trent, 1916

Below: Hewitt & Leadbeater willow pottery doll, dressed by a child, *Pollock's Toy Museum*

Below right: Two dolls of First World War period,
left: in Black Watch Tartan, unmarked, and
right: Hewitt & Leadbeater willow pottery, *Pollock's Toy Museum*

Facing: Advertisement in *The Toy Trader,* Dec 1922 and doll marked 'Dolly Dimple, Nunn & Smeed, Liverpool', made of pink bisque coated with wax, *Pollock's Toy Museum*

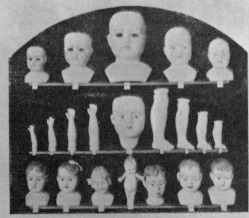

HEWITT & LEADBEATER,

SHOULDER AND SOCKET HEADS "CUT OUT" FOR FIXING OF GLASS EYES AND WIG.

BALD HEADS FOR FIXING WIG, WITH PAINTED EYES.

HEADS READY FOR FIXING TO THE BODY WITH PAINTED HAIR AND EYES.

ALL COLOURS ARE PERMANENT.

PRICES AND SIZES SENT ON APPLICATION.

THE MANUFACTURERS OF FINEST PORCELAIN DOLLS HEADS AND LIMBS.
WILLOW POTTERY, LONGTON, STOKE-ON-TRENT,
Also NORMACOT ROAD, LONGTON.

THE NONSUCH WALKING DOLLS

PATENTEES & SOLE MANUFACTURERS :

NUNN & SMEED,
BENLEDI STREET, LIVERPOOL.

Telegrams : "Nonsuch, Liverpool."   Telephone : Royal 2317.

Doll marked 'Gipsy—English
make', *Pollock's Toy Museum*

Below: Dolls' heads marked
'Melba', made by Mayer &
Sherratt, Longton, Staffs during
First World War, *Pollock's Toy
Museum*

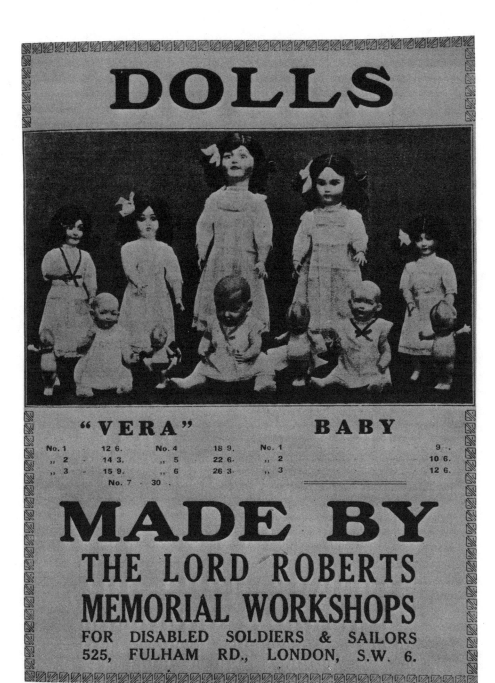

DOLLS

"VERA"   BABY

No. 1	12 6.	No. 4	18 9.	No. 1	9 -.
,, 2	14 3.	,, 5	22 6.	,, 2	10 6.
,, 3	15 9.	,, 6	26 3.	,, 3	12 6.
		No. 7	30 .		

MADE BY
THE LORD ROBERTS
MEMORIAL WORKSHOPS
FOR DISABLED SOLDIERS & SAILORS
525, FULHAM RD., LONDON, S.W. 6.

Above: Vera Dolls, as advertised in *The Toy Trader* for August 1913, by Keen & Co of London, a subsidiary of Kohnstam, a German firm. Claimed to be the first British-made jointed dolls (heads were imported from Germany).

Left: as advertised by Lord Roberts Memorial Workshops in April 1919. (Keen's were closed during the war as an enemy firm, and Lord Roberts' took the doll over.)

Below: From an advertisement by Whyte Ridsdale & Co, a large wholesaler, in 1915

Right: Hybrid dolls, *Pollock's Toy Museum;*
left: old leather body, repaired with a head marked Melba (Mayer & Sherratt)
right: a French Jumeau body, repaired with a head marked 'Classic—Cecily'

Below: The larger doll is marked 'Hamley's—hair—stuffed' on the body; the smaller 'GB—made in England' on the head, *Pollock's Toy Museum*

Facing: Toyland Dolls was an enterprise set up in Stoke-on-Trent in 1916 on the initiative of George Henry Buckmaster, manager of the local (Shelton) branch of WH Smith & Son, the giant firm of newsagents and stationers

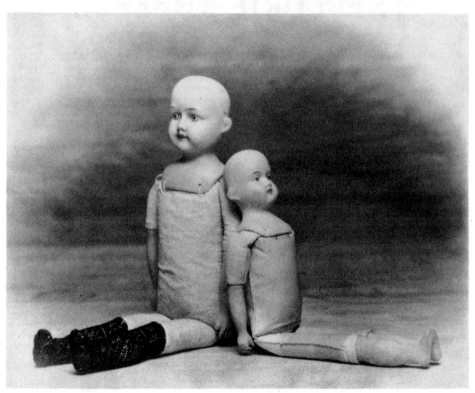

Enterprising ladies

The lace-making town of Nottingham was reputed to be the home of the prettiest girls in England, possibly because for generations women had gone out to work in the textile factories, and with the money they earned had been able to afford good food and clothes and to bring up their children in relative ease.

The outbreak of war in 1914 led to a great deal of unemployment among women. 'At this time, however'—to quote an article in *Games and Toys*— 'among certain people was displayed an admirable and courageous spirit of enterprise. Not the least important were those who were prompt to realise and profit from the opportunities disclosed for the toy industry by the complete cessation of German commerce. Credit should be given to Miss Wallis for her foresight, resolution and energy in starting the Nottingham Toy Industry.'

At first Miss Wallis, who appears to have been a well-to-do lady, concentrated on the manufacture of small rag dolls with a charming composition mask. Her next step was to ask a sculptor, Helen Fraser Rock, to design some china dolls' heads. Modelled from real children, these pioneer English china dolls were called Helen's Babies; and as the potters used an especially strong and solid material they were advertised as Rock China Dolls.

Miss Wallis next turned her attention to dolls' bodies, producing a featherweight 'compolite' body. These Daisy Dolls had four different pretty dresses: Queen Mary, visiting the British Industries Fair, particularly admired one wearing a simple muslin frock with a ribbon sash. Miss Wallis's Vogue dolls, however, had bodies made of leatherette, with china heads and arms; while their wardrobes were elaborate and most fashionable. Each year more lines were added to the range, including some cheaper Rock China Twins: Peter and Pauline, Joyce and Josylin. ·

Meanwhile in London the formidable Miss Muriel Moller opened her showroom for British toys at 110 Cheapside. She took under her wing not only the dolls designed by Helen Fraser Rock, but also those created by Mrs EE Houghton for the Shanklin Toy Industry, which had originated and evolved in the same sort of way as the Nottingham Toy Industry. Its cuddly stockinette dolls, all signed and numbered by Mrs Houghton, were carefully made and amusingly dressed by capable workers, first on a cottage industry scale in Shanklin, Isle of Wight, and later in a factory at Greenwich, London.

Outstanding, however, in sales and popularity during these war years were the long-legged, black-stockinged dolls designed by the prolific Hilda Cowan for the manufacturers and wholesalers Laurie Hansen and for the British Novelty Works, a subsidiary of Dean's Rag Book Company.

Waving the Flag—Dean's Patriotic
Rag Dolls

Printed fabric dolls, by Samuel
Finburgh, Manchester, (Reprinted
1970 by HM Stationery Office)
with Dean's Tru-to-Life rag doll in
pink undies

Tommy Atkins—rag doll sold by
Whyte Ridsdale, 1914

The Unconscious Doll Exerciser

This remarkable line (of which much has been heard) is now ready and buyers are invited to see samples immediately.

The Doll Exerciser will undoubtedly be one of the finest selling lines ever produced.

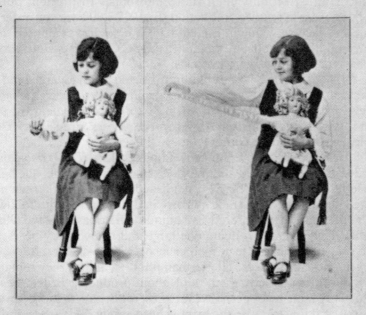

The demonstrations at the Savoy Hotel have created great interest and arrangements will be made for special displays and demonstrations at the leading London Stores.

The Dolls themselves—dressed as Red Cross Nurses and Boy Scouts—are beautifully modelled and a large chart of the various exercising games is provided with each.

LIBERAL DISCOUNT TO THE TRADE.

The ...tional Doll League, 64, Regent St., London, W.

Eugene Sandow's Exercise Doll, by the All-British Doll Manufacturing Co, Sheffield, 1917

Advertisement in *The Toy Trader* for plastolite dolls' heads and limbs, 1917

Misska dolls, by Art Toy Manufacturing Co, London, 1920

Teddy's Bear, after the original cartoon by Berryman

Facing: First World War bear as a wounded soldier, *Pollock's Toy Museum*

And resourceful businessmen

Toy bears—realistic brown Bruin bears, with all four paws firmly on the ground, have been in toy cupboards for probably over a century, but it was not until 1903 that the Teddy Bear was born.

In November 1902 a political cartoon appeared in the Washington Post showing Theodore Roosevelt refusing to shoot a bear cub while on a hunting expedition in Mississippi. The cartoon was so popular that prints were made of it; and subsequently, Teddy's bears followed the President wherever he went.

Morris Michtom, an enterprising small store owner in New York, cut out a plush toy based on the bear cub picture, and got the President's permission to call it 'Teddy Bear'. It was an instant success. Michtom's original bear now resides in dignified retirement in the Smithsonian Institution; but by 1903 'Teddy' bears were in regular production. By 1907 3,000 were on order from the German Steiff factory, while in England TB Richies had composed *The Teddy Bears' Picnic* (although it had to wait until a BBC Children's Hour broadcast in 1933 to have the familiar words added).

In the early years, the bears were hump-backed and had large hind legs, like real bears; but these features were soon abandoned as Teddy's characteristic shape developed. This 'humanised' form was more convenient for clothing a bear, and they rapidly acquired wardrobes. Bears dressed as clowns, in particular, enjoyed quite a vogue.

In 1908 Dean's published a half-crown book entitled *Teddy Bear*, and in 1909 two London firms printed cut-out fabric bears to sew at home, one being made of flannelette. 'The Teddy Bear has established a reputation that can never die', proclaimed the editor of a trade journal in 1908; and in the following year Morrell's of Oxford Street offered, as a unique Christmas novelty, 'Old mistress Teddy that lived in a Shoe, being one large and twelve baby bears, a sledge, ladder, bowls etc., and a fifteen inch crimson shoe'—all for 21s.

However, these bears were all German imports, and so they remained until the war induced manufacturers to think about producing British Bears. Of all the German toy industries, perhaps the easiest for Britain to capture was the soft toy industry, and in particular the by now burgeoning Teddy Bear industry; for

William Henry Jones, a pioneer of the British soft toy industry

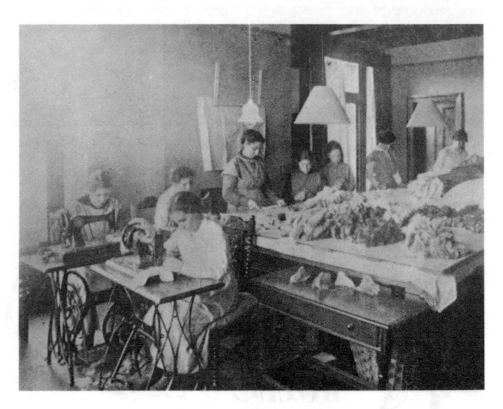

virtually no plant was required—basically, just a table and a sewing machine; and many, like the highly successful Mr Jones, began with just a few girls and a back room. Moreover, the materials were to hand. The mohair plush required for bearskins was made in Yorkshire, principally at Huddersfield and Dewsbury; and unlike most other raw materials it was neither rationed nor in short supply.

By 1916 The Star Manufacturing Company were proudly offering six sizes of bear with growlers; while Mark Robin of the Britannia Toy Works came out with Cossack, a bear dressed in Russian uniform and hat, which were described as giving it 'quite a unique appearance'. Then there were Hugg Mee bears, and Ally bears, and a curious vogue for ethereal creatures that were half bear and half doll, usually white.

Sawdust and wood wool were at first the principal stuffing materials: kapok largely replaced them in the early 1920s. Early bears saw the world through black metal boot buttons; later ones through glass eyes, made on a wire, which were originally manufactured for taxidermists. Birmingham was the centre of this trade; the eyes made there were not as fine as the German eyes, which were blown, but British manufacturers developed a method of making cheap flat, clear eyes, with the colouring painted in on the back.

After the war the soft toy manufacturers fared rather better than most. Soft toys had never been really cheap, so British firms were better able to compete with foreigners.

The teddy bear's arrival on the scene was well-timed. His birth coincided with a new appreciation of the role of the soft toy in a young child's development; while psychologists and educators were at one in attributing to toy animals, in particular, the virtue of soothing the savage infantile breast, and of inculcating a more affectionate attitude towards dumb beasts and other unfortunates.

Thus the Teddy Bear's survival was assured. Unlike the grotesques and the character dolls, the crazes and the fads which had their peaks of fashion, their critics, and their falls from favour, Teddy Bears were above reproach.

Right: 1917 Swan bears, made by Star Manufacturing Co, London

The peace and the years of depression

The end of fighting did not of course bring for the consumer any immediate and dramatic change in the supply of toys available in the shops. The consumer, however, could cheerfully survive the shortages, as personal memories of those times can testify.

From Tapioca for Tea, *by Sarah Shears*

'We used the front room every day now and not only on Sundays, and the presents were laid out for our inspection when we came home from school. The bicycles, costing the fabulous sum of seven guineas each, were being delivered later.

'The doll, for which I had longed so passionately when I was seven, was a little late to receive the affection she deserved, but I liked her well enough for another two years or so.

'"I had to visit every toyshop in town to find her, darling," Father explained, as I lifted her gently out of the long box. "You see, all the best dolls come from Germany, and we haven't imported any during the war, and still can't buy a German doll, for love or money. I'm sorry; but I'm afraid she has a false wig, and her eyes don't close, and her legs won't bend. Apparently she has to spend her days standing up, and go to sleep with her eyes open!'

'"It doesn't matter, she's b-beautiful", I assured him, and smothered him with grateful hugs and kisses.

'William, in the meantime, had raced upstairs with his air-gun, to practise shooting from a bedroom window, followed by Mother, urging him to be careful and not to shoot any birds.

'"Haven't we had enough of war and guns?" She spoke rather sharply to Father, because of her new anxiety.

'"My dear, it's as natural for a boy to want a gun, as a girl to want a doll", said Father complacently, as he laid out Mary's tea-set on the table, and pushed the wooden horse into Henry's reluctant hands'.

Sarah Shears, aged five

89

A GLASS EYED FOREIGNER WAS RECENTLY DISCOVERED GNAWING AT THE FOUNDATIONS OF BRITISH TRADE

Cartoon advertisement from *Games & Toys,*

Facing: Swords to ploughshares: Britain's Farm, *Pollock's Toy Museum*
inset: Advertisement, Prepare for Peace in *Games and Toys*

The problems of the toy trade

The lack of quality German dolls may have been regretted by customers: for the toy trade their return was disastrous. Already in 1917 *The Toy and Fancy Goods Trader* had been full of forebodings:

'If this Armageddon finished to-morrow it would be months, perhaps years, before effective protective legislation could be put into operation. Meanwhile the Germans would have resumed their grip on our markets as tenaciously as they did before hostilities commenced. There are thousands of men in England to-day who are ready to buy German goods from German firms the first moment they are offered. They put profit before everything.'

Nevertheless, on September 1st 1919 Lloyd George's government, respecting its Free Trade principles, lifted the restrictions on the import of foreign toys to Britain. Within a few years the victors' Reparations policies, and the economic sanctions consequent on their breakdown, intensified the malaise of the home industry. 'Crisis in British Trade', 'Tidal Wave of German Goods', 'Devaluation of the Mark and German Toy Dumping', proclaimed the headlines; while the conservative *Morning Post* attacked government policy by harping on the plight of disabled ex-servicemen:

'Now that we are on the verge of bankruptcy it is criminal folly to send out our money in return for toy trash . . . We also have a duty to our disabled ex-servicemen who are producing toys—not perhaps as cheap and showy as the German, but quite good enough for British children to play with. We are snatching the bread out of the ex-servicemen's mouths in order to give it to the people whose aim was—and is— to destroy us all . . . The toys these soldiers make are the only means left to them of living. If their toys are not bought, they starve.'

Letters to editors were full of advice and suggestions. A toy wholesaler, Mr Charles White, writes in 1921: 'Look at the lines on offer by the German houses. Practically all the dolls have been lying in damp warehouses, and although decay in the composition is not apparent on the surface, the limbs soon crumble and fall to pieces. Germany moreover to-day is without elastic or mohair. The only way to stop the English market being flooded is for British manufacturers to combine in a great advertising and publicity campaign.' Other readers pointed out that many foreign firms were finding ways of by-passing the new Merchandise Marks Act by stamping the packing cases or cartons with the country of origin, but not the individual toys; or by attaching to dolls made in Germany large labels describing them as 'English Dressed'.

There were no easy solutions, however, as the more percipient recognised. While there were complaints about the Board of Trade's minimum wage rates, no one wanted a return to the low wages and sweated labour of the 19th century. There was plenty of opposition, too, to any policy of relying on a protectionist tariff. There would always, in the opinion of these people, be a market for well-made, good quality toys; and there was no reason to fear foreign competition in areas where British manufacturers had always done well: lead soldiers, rag dolls, large wooden toys. And when, in 1921, the *Toy Trader* invited its readers to vote on whether German firms should be allowed to advertise in its pages, there was a large majority in favour.

There was, moreover, a certain inconsistency in the stance of the trade journals themselves. On one page a journal would lament that 'several wholesale houses have decided for the present to have nothing to do with German toys; but others, to whom patriotism means little or nothing, are attempting to snatch a quick profit by securing stocks of pre-war toys made by our late enemies and selling them at post-war prices.' Yet on the next page the same journal would recount admiringly how, for example, 'the King of the toy trade, Mr Joe Eisenmann, head of the wholesale import firm founded in Bavaria, has moved into spacious new premises in the City of London'; or how 'Mr Charles Luckman, after serving three years in the Navy, has set up in business, specialising in the import of dolls, and by 1921 has financed and taken the entire

PREPARE FOR
PEACE!

output of three doll factories in Sonneberg, Thuringia,' *The Toy Trader* adds, as if by way of justification that 'Mr Luckman is a diligent student of English fashion journals, and his dolls are dressed according to English styles in the latest modes.'

Meanwhile, what was happening to the British doll manufacturers? The *Toy Trader* writes in 1920: 'But for the Staffordshire potteries there would be no doll industry in this country to-day. And unless steps are taken there is a strong probability that the manufacture of dolls' heads will become a thing of the past. All the pottery firms are complaining about the "waiting game" practised by retailers, wholesalers and doll manufacturers. They are disgusted with the way the trade treats them—leaving orders till the last moment, returning stuff on the slightest provocation, or expecting them to accumulate huge stocks. Consequently, those continuing in the doll-head industry are providing themselves with the means of doing a constant by making complete china dolls.'

Mr JL Amberg, head of the great American toy firm, sounded another note of warning, however, when on a visit to London in 1924: 'Cost of production is prohibiting the making of bisque doll heads; and in recent years there has been a steadily decreasing demand for bisque or papier maché dolls. I prophesied in Germany four years ago that they would have to come to the "Mama" doll with a durable composition head—and I could not get a single manufacturer to even try to make one. But to-day a hundred factories are producing them—not to mention an indefinite quantity of home workers.'

Fragile, pretty, expensively-dressed china dolls were on their way out, as was the sheltered nursery life of the well-to-do little girls for whom they were bought and who played with them gently under the constant supervision of an ever-present nanny or nurserymaid. For the moment, in the early 1920s, there was security and prosperity for some, but it was ill shared out. Exhortations of the British Toy Manufacturers' Association, jeremiads in the press, royal visits to the British industry fairs did little to relieve the gloomy industrial climate—for toy makers as for others. The toy hawkers, sadly wearing their service medals, stood in the gutters of Holborn, and thousands of children grew up in penury far worse than Angela Rodaway's, and difficult now to imagine. One who knew their condition intimately (he was Honorary Treasurer of the Ragged School Union) was Mr Walter Scholes, head of the long-established toy firm of Wisbey's of Houndsditch. He told the London Rotary Club in August 1922 that 'the slum areas of London are almost a foreign land, in which tens of thousands of little human derelicts are living by their wits. There are over 150,000 children in London who are on the borderline of extreme poverty, and of these over 8,000 are cripples.'

Doing her Bit—a munitions girl doll, by The Dolls' Accessory Co 1919 and Where's Hubby? (Na-po series) by Hewitt Bros. Stoke-on-Trent

Right: Street Singers—illustration by E Farmiloe from *Rag, Tag and Bobtail* 1899

Queen Mary's Dolls' House

Queen Mary and, *below*, King George at the British Industries Fair, 1922

Queen Mary's Dolls' House

It is well to remember that there were many outside the reach even of Woolworth's stores. But a history of toys should be a celebration of things made, not a lament for deprivation; and in the 1920s all was not despondency—far from it. In 1924 a huge British Empire Exhibition was organised at Wembley: it attracted vast crowds, and businessmen from all over the world. One of the exhibits which drew everyone's delighted admiration was the splendid dolls' house designed for Queen Mary by Sir Edwin Lutyens, and which is now on show at Windsor Castle.

Over 16,000 people worked to create this house. Much of the furniture was made by Lines Brothers at their Ormside Street works, with the aid of microscopes and specially designed tools. Living artists of the day contributed

DAY NURSERY

NURSERY LOBB[Y]

MAN'S ROOM

QUEEN'S BATHROOM

QUEEN'S BEDROOM

QUEEN'S WARDRO[BE]

tiny oil paintings, prints and watercolours; while the miniature books which line the shelves of the library were specially written by their respective authors and form a complete survey of English literature for the year 1920. Furthermore, in the words of a contemporary account, 'every room is furnished as fully as if it were required for actual use. The kitchens are equipped with ranges, dressers, tables, shelves, and every conceivable domestic utensil. In the pantries are exquisite dinner and tea services, and a complete and valuable miniature coffee service of silver.

'Tiny switches control the electric light. Running water, obtained from specially constructed cisterns, supplies the sculleries and bathrooms, which are fitted with silver taps. Electric lifts convey visitors in imagination from floor to floor.

'Outside, there is a wonderful garage in which are housed three perfect model motor cars, and a motor cycle and sidecar. There are inspection pits, workshops and living accommodation for the imaginary chauffeur.'

Queen Mary's Dolls' House, and Lines Brothers' part in it, can in spite of the setbacks of the early twenties very properly, and encouragingly, represent the British toy industry in the middle of the decade; for as we have seen, 1925 marks the beginning of an unprecedented growth in its prosperity and standing.

Queen Mary's Dolls' House at Windsor Castle. Reproduced by gracious permission of Her Majesty The Queen

95

Princess Victoria aged ten, from a picture by William Fowler

QUEEN VICTORIA'S DOLLS

Looking back

In 1894 Frances H Low wrote for the Strand Magazine an article on Queen Victoria's dolls. It brought her such a fan mail that she hastened to expand it into a book, which was duly published with the seal of royal approval by George Newnes the same year. A second article in the Strand followed: *Distinguished Women and their Dolls*. We know nothing further of the writer, but gratefully acknowledge our indebtedness both to her, since it is from her pages that nearly the whole of this section derives, and to Alan Wright, the illustrator of *Queen Victoria's Dolls*.

From Queen Victoria's Dolls, *by Frances H Low*

'Her Majesty was very much devoted to dolls, and indeed played with them till she was nearly fourteen years old. Her favourites were small dolls—small wooden dolls, which she could occupy herself with dressing.

'The dolls are of the most unpromising material, and would be regarded with scorn by the average Board School child of to-day, whose toys, thanks to modern philanthropists, are often of the most extravagant and expensive description. Whether expensive dolls were not obtainable at that period, or whether the Princess preferred these droll little wooden creatures as more suitable for the representation of historical and theatrical personages, I know not; but the whole collection is made up of them; and they certainly make admirable little puppets, being articulated at the knees, thigh joints, elbows and shoulders, and available for every kind of dramatic gesture and attitude.

'It must be admitted that they are not aesthetically beautiful with their Dutch doll—not Dutch—type of face. Occasionally, owing to a chin being a little more pointed, or a nose a little blunter, there is a slight variation of expression; but with the exception of height, which ranges from three inches to nine inches, they are precisely the same. There is the queerest mixture of infancy and matronliness in their little wooden faces, due to the combination of small, sharp noses and bright vermilion cheeks (consisting of a big dab of paint in one spot) with broad, placid brows, over which, neatly parted on each temple, are painted

Princess Victoria, from a picture painted in 1830 by Richard Westall RA

Below: Nina Lady Norton in crimson silk dress with white rosettes and
Sir William Arnold, wearing green trousers and a blue waistcoat under a long lawn overcoat

elaborate, elderly, greyish curls. The remainder of the hair is coal black, and is relieved by a tiny yellow comb perched upon the back of the head.

'Of the 132 dolls preserved the Queen herself dressed no fewer than thirty-two, in a few of which she was helped by her governess Baroness Lehzen. They are for the most part theatrical personages and court ladies, and include also three males (of whom there are only seven or eight in the whole collection). The workmanship in the frocks is simply exquisite: tiny ruffles are shown with fairy stitches; wee pockets on aprons (it must be borne in mind these were for dolls of five or six inches only) are delicately finished off with minute bows; little handkerchiefs not more than half-an-inch square are embroidered with red silk initials; there are chatelaines of white and gold beads so small that they almost slip out of one's hands in handling; and one is struck afresh by the deftness of finger and the unwearied patience that must have possessed the youthful fashioner.

'There is indeed ample evidence in the care and attention lavished on the dolls of the immense importance with which they were regarded by their royal little mistress; and an additional and interesting proof of this is to be found in what one might call the "dolls' archives". These records are to be found in an ordinary copy-book, now a little yellow with years, on the inside cover of which is written in a childish, straggling, but determined handwriting: "List of my Dolls". Then follows in delicate feminine writing the name of the doll, by whom it was dressed, and the character it represented, though this particular is sometimes omitted. When the doll represents an actress, the date and name of the ballet are also given, by means of which one is enabled to determine the date of the dressing—which must have been between 1831 and 1833, when the dolls were "packed away" '.

For anyone to whom 'Victorian' signifies 'strait-laced' or 'puritanical', the number of actresses, singers and dancers who feature among these dolls may come as a surprise. Amy Robsart from *Kenilworth*, Count Almaviva from *The Barber* and *Figaro*, and Bellini's *Sonnambula* are all there; there too is the celebrated dancer Marie Taglioni, portrayed in a variety of roles. For Queen Victoria's childhood was, of course, pre-'Victorian', still 'Regency' in style and

99

manners; and like almost everyone else then, she adored the theatre. As Frances Low reflects, 'The number and variety of her Liliputian mummers set one wondering whether the Princess had a miniature theatre, and if so whether she arranged her puppets simply as lay figures in tableaux, or whether they acted their parts in make-believe speech and gesture. What a fascinating picture it is of the little painted cardboard theatre, and what an enviable post for a stage manager! No discontented "stars", nor fault-finding critics, nor ill-mannered audience, but the most docile and manageable company of lace-bespangled ladies and gentlemen, and the politest of fashionable audiences, composed of becomingly-attired court ladies in the stalls.'

Mrs Keeley, the veteran actress, talks to Frances Low

'You ask me, in my eighty-seventh year, to remember the dolls of my childhood. Well, I'll try, but I fear the description will be very uninteresting. I never had but one doll—a great, heavy, wooden doll: no stuffing, no nice soft leather arms and legs. No, its limbs were strongly wedged, and pegged into its body; and it was so big and heavy I could scarcely drag it about (I was four years old only). Its name was Lummox. It was a nuisance to everybody in the house, and one unlucky day I let it fall upon my mother's foot, and in her pain and anger she put it on the kitchen fire, and there was an end of Lummox.'

Mrs Stanley, wife of the famous explorer

'The real interest and occupation of those "laughing days" was making our paper doll family. We began their manufacture at three years old, and continued till our teens. My sister and I, we each had a family consisting of a mother and thirteen children. These were drawn and coloured on stiff paper, and carefully cut out; the adults measuring about three inches, the children varying according to age. Each child had its particular cast of features, expression and colouring. As the paper dolls got torn, or soiled, or crumpled, two hours daily were spent in renovating the family. We were always careful to keep the likeness, so that each member was recognisable, though attired in some new dress. We had a special box for the family in evening dress, so that if an invitation came suddenly our dolls were always ready to appear in fashionable attire. We also had a supply of walking dresses, hats, cloaks, muffs and tippets. There was even a reserve of bathing costumes for when the family went down to the seaside (a soup-plate of water), but they could never remain long in the water, the colour coming off and the dolls becoming pulpy if too long immersed.'

The child who was to become Queen of England, and the girl who was to become Mrs Stanley, may have been ill-served by modern standards in the nursery (though they more than compensated by their imagination and their patience), but one precious commodity they did have: time. Children growing up in poverty had not even this: their days of childhood were days of drudgery too.

Ironically, Lucy Luck's early life was particularly unfortunate (her story is told in *Useful Toil: Autobiographies of Working People from 1820-1920*, edited by John Burnett). Orphaned very young, her home was the workhouse; at less than nine years old, she was already working a twelve-hour day in the silk-mills.

From the autobiography of Lucy Luck, a straw-plait worker

'I had to make five yards of straw plait every night after I had done work at the silk-mill. But I had a very good time with Mrs H. I don't ever remember one of them raising a hand to strike me. The Parish supplied my clothes: fairly good of the sort. I never remember having anything but cotton dresses, the old-fashioned lilac print capes like our dresses in the summer, and shawls in the winter; good strong petticoats and thick nailed boots, both summer and winter; big coal-scuttle bonnets, with a piece of ribbon straight across them. I leave you to guess what we looked like. I only remember having one plaything and that was a big doll that my sister had left me when she died.'

Early 19th century wooden doll, English, *Victoria & Albert Museum*

Facing: White Ayrshire needlework.
In 1814 a Scots lady, Mrs Jamieson, opened a small workshop in which she employed local girls to copy an embroidered baby's dress she had brought home from France. Soon thousands of women and quite young children were engaged in the manufacture of Ayrshire sewed muslin—weaving the cotton, spinning the yarn for embroidery, bleaching, ironing, and packing the finished 'white work' into fancy paper boxes and baskets. In Glasgow alone there were forty manufacturing houses; and in the whole of Scotland more than 25,000 'flowerers' earned their living stitching elegant flower and foliage designs on to collars, handkerchiefs, ruffles, edgings, and trimmings for shawls and dresses. By 1850, the fashion for light, simple muslin dresses had given way to heavy crinoline dresses, profusely trimmed with broderie anglaise and machine-made lace.

Toy traders

The 19th century saw a vast expansion of retail trading in all Britain's industrial cities, reflecting the rapid increase in population and in earnings, and the growth of international commerce. By the 1820s and 1830s smart new shops were proliferating in the West End of London, but these of course were for the well-to-do only. For ordinary working people most buying and selling took place in the street still; though street traders, particularly if dealing in perishables, increasingly set up their stalls within the protection of covered markets. The bazaar was coming into its own.

There was recognition, too, of children as part of the new consumer public; but for the vast majority of them, cheapness was all. The lengths to which an independent manufacturer, untrammeled by any public health regulation, might go in catering for children's needs, are vividly conveyed in the story of this sweet-maker's apprentice, taken from *Autobiographies of Working People, 1820-1920*:

William, a sweet-maker's apprentice

'I've seen him pretty well down and out—he had nothing but his coat and vest and I've taken it to the pawnbroker's and I've got two-and-six on the coat and vest and I've bought sugar at a penny a pound and a ha'penny a pound, because those days you used to buy scrapings out of the windows—sugar that was

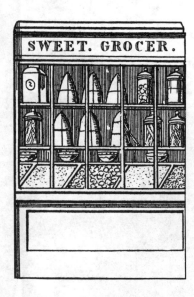

A scene from *Harlequin & the Giant Helmet,* in JK Green's toy theatre edition, 1841

Right: A scene from *Jack the Giant Killer,* JK Green, 1854

Facing: A scene from *Harlequin Red Riding Hood,* W Webb, 1858 and from *Harlequin St George,* JK Green, 1847

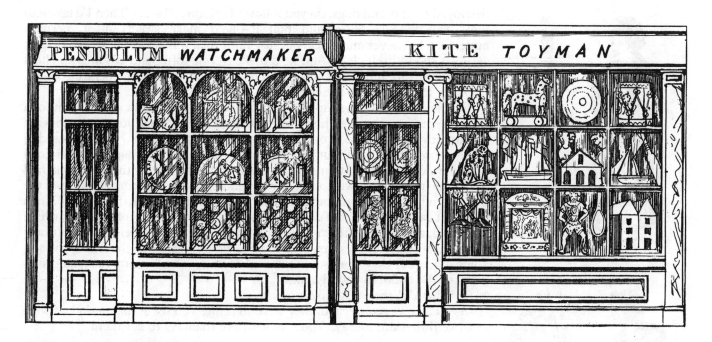

PENDULUM *WATCHMAKER*   KITE *TOYMAN*

destroyed by cats and dogs, do you follow? Flyblow, all sorts. Then I'd take it to
him. You follow? He would boil it—he'd make sweets of it, perhaps
butterscotch—never mint rock, because mint rock was always clear. It had to be
clean. It shows itself clear. And he'd make treacle toffee and all kinds and he'd
send me out with it to sell it and I used to sell it for tuppence ha'penny a pound.

Q. On the streets, or to shops?

'On the streets—or to shopkeepers. And those shopkeepers would sell it for a
penny a quarter. I've seen him make chocolate sticks. Have you ever seen what
the kiddies used to have at one time—a dear little toffee stick? Well, he used to
make those about . . . about twelve inches long and perhaps half an inch
diameter. Well, we used to make chocolate sticks of those by the simple method
of buying a pound or two pound of wax candles, extracting the wicks out of the
wax and buying brown umber and mixing brown umber with the wax until such
time as it came the colour of chocolate. And then he'd get the toffee sticks, which
were cold, and he'd dip them in this mixture, and with their being cold naturally
a certain quantity of the wax, or if you like what he said was chocolate, you see,
stuck to it. And they were sold as chocolate sticks, at a farthing each, ha'penny
each, to the children round about.

Q. What did they taste like?

'As far as I was concerned, they were all right. You see at that period we were
not like things are to-day. You see, we were thankful to get them.'

Street trading

Many of the characters whose working lives are recorded in Mayhew's *London*
were street traders catering particularly for the child market:

'Dolls are now cheap,' Mayhew observes, 'and so generally sold by open-air
traders whose wares are of a miscellaneous character. The dolls are most usually
carried in baskets by street sellers who are not makers, and generally by women
who are very poor. If the vendor can only attract the notice of children—and
more specially in a private suburban residence, where children are not used to
the sight of dolls on stalls or barrows, or in shops—and can shower a few
blessings and compliments, "God be wid your bhutiful faces then—and yors
too, my lady, ma'am (with a curtsey to mistress or maid). Buy one of these dolls
of a poor woman: shure they're bhutiful dolls, and shuted for them angels o'the
worruld", under such circumstances, I say, a sale is almost certain.'

'There are many articles which, having become cheap in the shops, find their
way to the street traders, and after a brief and prosperous trade has been carried
on in them, gradually disappear. Among such are the elastic toys called "gutta-
percha heads", these, however, have no gutta-percha in their compostition, but
are solely made of glue and treacle. The heads are small coloured models of the
human face, usually with projecting nose and chin, and wide or distorted mouth,
which admit of being squeezed into a different form of features, their elasticity
causing them to return to the original caste.

'Trade in crackers and detonating balls, I am informed by persons familiar
with it, would be much more frequently carried on by street-folk, were it not the
one which of all street callings finds the least toleration from the police. "You
must keep your eyes on both corners of the street", said one man, "when you sell
crackers; and what good is it the police stopping us? The boys have only to go to a
shop, and it's all right".

'The trade is principally carried on for a few days before and after the fifth of
November, and again at Christmastide. "Last November was good for
crackers", said one man. "I took 15s in a day, and nearly all off boys, for waterloo
crackers and ball crackers. I sold them from a barrow, wheeling it about as if it
was hearthstone, and just saying quietly when I could, 'Six a penny crackers'.
The boys soon tell one another."'

We are in mid-century, with the 'Peelers' in full swing and gradually applying
the relentless pressure on street traders which was eventually to drive most of
them, and their customers, into places where they were more easily controlled.

104

Thomas Spencer, born 1852,
Marks's partner
Top: Michael Marks, born 1862, in
his early thirties.

Left: Pedlar doll with kid head,
wooden body, red cloak, made
about 1830
Victoria & Albert Museum

Facing: From a toy theatre sheet of *Tricks for the Harlequinade,* published by W West, 1822. Surrounding it are characters from Skelt's *Harlequin and Old Dame Trot* and Redington's *Baron Münchausen*

The transfer of trading from the street to the open, or better the covered, market brought great advantages to the trader also. The most momentous day in the early career of Michael Marks, founder of Marks and Spencer, was the day when, from peddling his wares round the Yorkshire dales, he set up his stall in the open market at Kirkgate, in Leeds. The day his business really took wing was the day he moved again, into the covered market hall.

That was in the mid-eighties; and by that time covered markets, rather like the enormous department stores which were often called bazaars, had for decades been a feature of many large cities.

The Soho Bazaar

Thomas Allen, in his *History and Antiquities of London,* published in 1828, describes the Soho Bazaar as 'a very extensive, novel and curious establishment, founded by John Trotter esquire, a gentleman of considerable opulence and respectability residing in this place. The premises are very commodious and spacious, containing a space of nearly 300 feet by 130, from the Square to Dean Street on one hand and to Oxford Street on the other; consisting of several rooms, conveniently and comfortably fitted up with handsome mahogany counters. The walls are hung with red cloth, and at the end are large mirrors, a conspicuous clock, and fireplaces. The principal sale is jewellery, toys, books, prints, millinery, etc, and is conducted entirely by females.'

Charles Hindley's *Life and Times of James Catnach* adds the information that the bazaar has accommodation for upwards of 160 tenants; that at the end of one room is 'a large recess, occupied with a rustic aviary, through which runs a stream of water'; and that 'the bazaar has been frequently patronised by royalty'. Breaking into verse, he goes on:

'Ladies in furs, and gem'men in spurs,
   Who lollop and lounge about all day:
The bazaar in Soho is completely the go—
   Walk into the shop of Grimaldi!
     Come from afar, here's the bazaar,
     But if you wont deal with us, stay where you are.

'Here's rouge to give grace to an old woman's face,
   Trousers of check for a sailor;
Here's a cold ice, if you pay for it twice,
   And here's a hot goose for a tailor.
     Soho Bazaar, come from afar,
     Sing ri fal de riddle, and tal de ral la.'

And so on—and on. A posher place, clearly, than Marks's Penny Bazaar in Leeds—the germ of a future Harrods, rather than of 'Marks and Sparks': But it is Marks and Sparks who, give or take a few yards, occupy the site today.

The open air survivors

If toy traders were increasingly moving under cover, others sought after by the young still had the open air as their kingdom. The telescope exhibitor, for instance, whose estimate to Mayhew of his annual earnings was £125—by night; by day he worked as a tailor. Or the peep-show operator, whose scenes, according to his testimony, were 'mostly upon recent battles and murders. People is werry fond of the battles in the country, but a murder what is well known is worth more than all the fights. There was more took with Rush's murder than there has been even by the Battle of Waterloo itself.

'I've got many different plays to my show. There's *The Dog of Montargis* and the *Forest of Bondy;* there's the *Forty Thieves* (that never done no good to me); *The Devil and Dr Faustus;* and at Christmas we exhibit pantomimes.'

But above all there was Punch and Judy, quite severed now from its Italian origins and developing, from the early years of the century, the style, characters and story-line which, unmistakeably English, are still traditional to-day.

Image Man from *Harlequin and Old Dame Trot,* published by M & M Skelt for the toy theatre, 1837-40

106

Dollmakers

Memoirs of a London Doll

The operation of the cottage industry of dollmaking in the mid-19th century is nowhere more charmingly evoked than in the *Memoirs of a London Doll, written by herself*, edited by Mrs Fairstar, otherwise Richard Henry Horne, and published in 1846.

'In a large, dusky room', begins the first chapter, *My Making and my Birth*, 'at the top of a dusky house in one of the dusky streets of High Holborn, there lived a poor dollmaker, whose name was Sprat. His family consisted of his wife and three children—two boys and a girl.' The family's single room, serving as workshop by day, bedroom by night, is described, and the bench covered with the tools and materials of the family trade; then the narrative continues:

'All the family worked at doll-making, and were very industrious. Mr Sprat was of course the great manager and doer of most things, and always the finisher; but Mrs Sprat was also clever in her department, which was entirely that of the eyes. She either painted the eyes or else, for the superior class of dolls, fitted in the glass ones. She moreover always painted the eyebrows, and was so used to it that she could make exactly the same sort of arch when it was late in the evening and nearly dark, before candles were lighted. The eldest boy painted hair, or fitted and glued hair on to the heads of the best dolls. The second boy fitted half legs and arms together, by pegs at the joints. The little girl did nothing but paint rosy cheeks and lips, which she always did very nicely, though sometimes she made them rather too red, and looking as if very hot, or blushing extremely.

'Now Mr Sprat was very ingenious and clever in his business as a dollmaker. He was able to make dolls of various kinds, even of wax, or a sort of composition, and sometimes he did make a few of these; but his usual business was to make jointed dolls—dolls who could move their legs and arms in many positions—, and these of course were made of wood. Of this latter material I was manufactured.

'The first thing I recollect of myself was a kind of a pegging, and pushing, and scraping, and twisting, and tapping down at both sides of me, above and below. These latter operations were the fitting of my legs and arms. Then I passed into the hands of the most gentle of all the Sprat family, and felt something delightfully warm laid upon my cheeks and mouth. It was the little girl who was

From *Memoirs of a London Doll*, 1846

108

Above and left: Unmarked wax dolls, *Pollock's Toy Museum*

painting me a pair of rosy cheeks and lips, and her face as she bent over me was the first of life that my eyes distinctly saw. The face was a smiling one, and as I looked up at it I tried to smile too; but I felt some hard material over the outside of my face, which my smile did not seem to be able to get through, so I do not think the little girl perceived it.

'But the last thing done to me was by Mr Sprat himself, whose funny white face and round eyes I could now see. He turned me about and about in his hands, examining and trying my legs and arms, which he moved backwards and forwards, and up and down, to my great terror, and fixed my limbs in various attitudes. I was so frightened! I thought he would break something off me. However nothing happened, and when he was satisfied that I was a complete doll in all parts, he hung me up on a line that ran along the room overhead, extending from one wall to the other, and near to the two beams that also extended from wall to wall. I hung upon the line to dry, in company with many other dolls, both boys and girls, but mostly girls. The tops of the beams were also covered with dolls, all of whom, like those on the lines, were waiting there till their paint or varnish had properly dried and hardened. I passed my time in observing what was going on in the room under my line, and also the contents of the room, not forgetting my numerous little companions, who were all smiling and staring, or sleeping, around me.'

Wooden doll with waxed face,
1860, *Worthing Museum*

The maker of dolls' heads

With Mayhew (reporting in *The Morning Chronicle*, Letter 39) there is, as always, no sentimentalising: we are confronted at once with the harsh reality:

'His whole appearance showed grinding poverty. His cheeks were sunken, and altogether he seemed, from grief and care, like a man half dead. His room was bare of anything to be called furniture, except only a very poor bed, a chair or two, and a table or bench at which he was at work with his paste and paper. In one corner was an oblong object, covered with an old quilt. It was a coffin containing the body of his child, a girl four years old, who had died of the whooping cough. There were four living children in the room—all up, late as it was, and all looking feeble, worn and sickly. The man's manner was meek and subdued as he answered my questions.

'"I make the composition heads for the dolls—nothing else. They are made of papier maché (paper mashed, he called it). After they go out of my hands to the dollmakers, they are waxed. First, they are done over in 'flake' light (flesh colour), and then dipped in wax. I make a mould from a wax model, and in it work the paper—a peculiar kind of sugar paper.

'"My little girl, fifteen years old, and myself can only make twelve or thirteen dozen a day of the smallest heads. For them I get 4s the gross, and the material, I reckon, costs me 1s 10d. If I make 2s 6d a day I reckon it is a good day's work—and what is half-a-crown for such a family as mine?

'"My wife makes a few dolls' arms of stuffed sheepskin: sawdust is used. She only gets seven farthings a dozen for them, and has very little employment. My trade used to be far better: now they get the bodies stuffed with sawdust at 2s 6d a gross, and they used to pay 5s. It's starvation work, stuffing 144 bodies for half-a-crown. Ah sir, the children of the people who will be happy with my dolls little think under what circumstances they are made, nor do their parents—I wish they did."'

The maker of dolls' eyes

In answer to Mayhew again:

'"I make all kinds of eyes, both dolls' and human eyes: the birds' eyes are mainly manufactured in Birmingham. Of dolls' eyes there are two sorts: the common and the natural, as we call it. The common are simply small hollow glass spheres, made of white enamel, and coloured either black or blue. The natural ones are made in a superior manner. You see this blue one: it has the iris correctly represented.

'"A man may make about twelve dozen pairs of the commoner, and about two or three dozen pairs of the better ones, in the course of a day. Average it throughout the year, a journeyman dolls'-eye maker earns about 30s a week.

'"Where we make one pair of eyes for home consumption, we make ten for exportation. I make eyes for a French house at Havre that exports a vast quantity. The eyes that we make for Spanish America are all black: a blue-eyed doll in that country wouldn't sell at all. Here, however, nothing goes down but blue eyes. The reason for this is because that's the colour of the Queen's eyes, and she sets the fashion in this as in other things.

'"We also make human eyes. Here are two cases—one black and hazel, and the other blue and grey". He then took the lids off a couple of boxes that stood on the table; they each contained 190 different eyes and so like nature that the effect produced upon a person unaccustomed to the sight was most peculiar and far from pleasant. "Here, you see", he continued, taking one from the blue-eye tray, "are the ladies' eyes. You see it's clearer, and not so bilious as the gentleman's. There's more sparkle and brilliance about it. Here's two different ladies' eyes— fine looking young women both of them. When a lady or gentleman comes to us for an eye we are obliged to have a sitting, just like a portrait painter. We take no sketch, but study the tint of the perfect eye.

'"I suppose we make from 300 to 400 false eyes every year. The human eyes are part blown and part cast, and we are obliged to be very good chemists to know the action of the metallic oxides on the fire, so as to produce the proper colour of the iris. Our usual price is £2 2s for one of our best.'"

Bazzoni's talking doll

Mayhew also records a statement made to him, apparently, by M Bazzoni, a tradesman in High Holborn:

'"I am the only person who ever made the speaking doll. I make her say 'papa' and 'mama'. I haven't one in the house to show you now. I have sold the last. I sold one to be sent to St. Petersburg: it was damaged on the passage, and when landed couldn't say either 'papa' or 'mama', and the gentleman who bought it couldn't get it mended in all Russia. I could have told him that before.

Trade card from the Guildhall Library

THE

SPEAKING DOLL!

A. BAZZONI,

MANUFACTURER OF WAX & COMPOSITION DOLLS,

AND

Maker of the Speaking-Doll,

No. 128,

High Holborn.

RESPECTFULLY informs the juvenile portion of the Female Nobility, Gentry, and the Public, that after a succession of experiments, he has finally succeeded in imparting the wonderful Faculty of SPEECH to his DOLLS, which for neatness of Workmanship, and elegance of Costume, defy competition. For the unprecedented patronage with which he has been honoured, he returns his grateful acknowledgments; it will be his undeviating study to merit a continuance of their kind Favours.

LINES ON THE SPEAKING DOLL.

In modern times "Inventions" are the rage,
And scheming minds in mighty tasks engage;
Steam-boats, Steam-couching, and the brilliant blaze
Of Gas, are wonders of these pregnant days;
Newspapers, too, the terror of bad Kings,
Are work'd by Steam, as swift as Morning's wings,
Old England's glory is maintain'd by vapour,
And Steam will keep it longer than her Paper.
Blest Peace continue our fair Isle to guard,
The Arts to prosper, Genius to reward;
If Foes should threaten, soon they'd be undone,
They'd dread the pow'r of our Percussion Gun.
No plan like this e'er mov'd Bazzoni's mind,
To Peace and Arts from infancy inclin'd.
In nightly study its sole aim to reach—
His DOLLS have now the Faculty of SPEECH!
They are as comely, and as bright and fair,
As e'er was Beauty in the balmy air;

With modest aspect charm the raptur'd sight,
And many a Miss has kiss'd them with delight.
"Papa!" "Mama!" his little Nymphs exclaim,
And with their own proclaim their maker's fame.
Unlike those figures which were made of old,
Unseemly shap'd, and in their features bold,
Mere rough-hewn blocks, like Otaheite's Gods,
Before whose Majesties that nation nods!
Ye rising Fair, to Merit give its due,
Bazzoni's Art has giv'n a Treat to you.
Nature his copy, he has giv'n it just—
The perfect semblance of the human bust.
And what sweet Miss in all her blooming charms
Would not embrace his Smilers in her arms?
For to be sage, the Muse (though rather droll),
Infers that Miss who "dearly doats" on Doll,
Imbibes a love, as tender as 'tis true,—
A love to kindred which is justly due!

LEWIS AND CO. PRINTERS, 96, BUNHILL ROW.

111

Queen Victoria drew and etched this portrait of herself with her first baby

Facing: A doll thought to be modelled on Princess Beatrice, perhaps by Montanari

Inset: A wax doll of c 1857, with similar characteristics, *Pollock's Toy Museum*

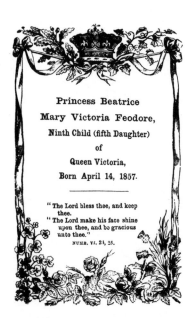

Princess Beatrice
Mary Victoria Feodore,
Ninth Child (fifth Daughter)
of
Queen Victoria,
Born April 14, 1857.

"The Lord bless thee, and keep thee.
"The Lord make his face shine upon thee, and be gracious unto thee."
NUMB. VI. 24, 25.

From *The Child's Companion*

'"The invention of the speaking doll took me many experiments and much study. The thought first struck me one day on hearing a penny trumpet—why not make a doll speak? Science is equal to everything. Some time ago a ventriloquist came over from Dublin to me: he could imitate everything but a baby, and he came to consult me about a baby's voice. I put him in my showroom and said, 'You stand in the corner and hear it.' I made the doll speak, and he said, 'That is the thing.' He gave two guineas for the price of the machine (not a doll), and went away quite glad. I have taken the apparatus to a party and made him speak on the stairs: a young gentleman I did it to tease turned quite white, as he could not tell who or what was coming.

'"After I determined to manufacture a speaking doll, I persevered day by day, thinking of it when doing other things, and completed it in three months. I sell rather more than a dozen in a year, at £6 6s each. Many a time in my showroom have the children looked out for the baby when they heard my doll. I had a rascal of a parrot once who could say 'papa' and 'mama as well as my doll herself—the parrot learnt it from the doll.

'"Many dollmakers have dissected my speaking doll to get at my secret. I know one clever man who tried twelve months to copy it, and then he put his work in the fire!"'

This statement gives away no trade secrets, and some of its narrative is a little confusing. M Bazzoni was evidently an excellent publicist, but neither Mr Mayhew nor anyone else of whom we have record is known for sure to have possessed or even to have seen this doll. It is perhaps unworthy to speculate that M Bazzoni may always 'just have sold the last one', but we would welcome reassurance on the point!

The baby doll: a late developer

The artists of the Renaissance, who mastered representational techniques and painted what they saw with a realism unknown for a thousand years, depicted the infant Jesus with chubby, life-like baby features. And what more appropriate? For the more total the babe's innocence and helplessness, the more telling the miracle of God incarnate.

The infant doll, however, continued for centuries to be an adult in miniature. A plaything in the likeness of a real baby was unknown before the 19th century, developed only gradually during it, and not mass-produced till the Edwardian age. Why not, one wonders?

One answer is that until children came to be regarded as people of significance in their own right, and not just apprentice adults, it was not to be expected that child dolls, whether intended for children or for adults, would be given child-like features. Alternatively, it could be that in a predominantly rural society of large families (if not normally many survivors) children would be surrounded by, and have to help mind and care for, an annual succession of live babies, in whose company artificial ones would be superfluous; and that only when growing children were hived off into the shelter of the nursery could baby dolls, realistically designed, earn their place among playthings as a source of delight.

In England, Queen Victoria's passionate interest in babies may have given this trend to greater realism its initial impulse. Osborne house, her holiday home in the Isle of Wight, is still littered with marble infants' limbs; and the birth of her first baby was a strong incentive to wax doll makers like the Montanari and Pierotti families to design and produce Royal Babies.

These dolls, like those made in Germany by Motschmann in 1855, had rather chubby limbs, attached to a stuffed cloth body, slightly shaped. If they were large enough they could be dressed in a real baby's long gowns and nightdresses; otherwise, useful hours could be spent learning to sew miniature layettes. China heads with features modelled on new-born babies, attached to dimpled papier maché composition bodies, were not however mass-produced until Edwardian times.

Right: Wax fashion doll by HJ
Meech, 'dollmaker to the royal
family', London, 1883, *Worthing
Museum*

Below: Doll's pram, c 1880 *Pollock's
Toy Museum*

Toymakers

An overall view

Mayhew's Letter XXXVII to the *Morning Chronicle* on the theme of Labour and the Poor, dated 21st February 1850, examines the situation of the metropolitan toymakers. The list he draws up of the 'arts and artists' involved in the manufacture of toys testifies to an enormous range of tiny cottage industries, the unit being as often as not a single family:

'There is the turner, to turn the handles of the skipping ropes, the ninepins, the peg, humming and whipping tops, the hoop-sticks; the basket-worker, to make dolls' cradles, and babies' rattles, and wicker-work carts and carriages; the tinman, to manufacture tin swords and shields, pea-shooters and carts, money-boxes, and miniature candlesticks; the pewterer, to cast the metal soldiers, dolls' cups and saucers, fire-irons, knives and forks, plates and dishes, chairs and tables, and all the leaden furniture of the baby-house; the modeller, to make the skin and composition animals; the glassblower, to make the dolls' eyes; the wig maker, to manufacture dolls' curls; the tallow-chandler, to mould miniature candles for the dolls' houses; the potter, to produce dolls' cups and saucers. Then there are image-men, conjurors, cutlers, cardmakers, opticians, cabinet-makers, firework-makers—and indeed almost every description of artisan, for there is scarcely a species of manufacture or handicraft that does not contribute something to the amusement of the young.'

Mayhew goes on to hazard some statistics. He estimates the number of toymakers and dealers in Britain at 1,866, of whom roughly one half were in the Birmingham area and one quarter in the metropolitan. By a rough and ready calculation he arrives at a figure of about £44,000 as their estimated annual earnings; £156,000 as the total value of the toys sold in Britain in a year; and 4¼d as the average amount spent on toys annually by each young person (aged under 20). No doubt a modern statistician could drive a coach and horses through these figures, but at least they serve to remind us of the substantial value of a penny in mid-19th century Britain!

More interesting, perhaps, is Mayhew's figure of £22,000 as the valuation put by Customs on the toys imported to Britain in the year under consideration (1841). This is only one-sixth of his figure for domestic production; and even allowing for a wide margin of error it provides some corrective to the impression created by a study of the toys which have *survived* from that period—the impression that Britain relied mainly on the continent to supply her with toys. It reminds us that for every child having toys whose value was counted in shillings or pounds, a hundred had nothing costing more than a penny; and that the overwhelming majority of penny toys were produced domestically. This remained broadly true even after 1842, when a cut in the import levy brought a lot of complaints of unfair foreign competition and no doubt contributed something, though less than they thought, to the hardships experienced by many of the toymakers whom Mayhew interviewed.

Mayhew concludes his report with some observations by a substantial Holborn toy dealer on the strengths and weaknesses of the British toy industry by comparison with its continental rivals:

'None, in my opinion, can be compared to the French in the ingenuity of their toys: they surpass the skill of the English workman. I am convinced, indeed, that the English toymaker can hardly so much as repair a broken French toy. Few watch-makers here can repair a clock-work mouse; they will generally charge 2s 6d for repairing a mechanical mouse that I sell new for 3s 6d. Such a mouse could not be made here, if it could be made at all, for less than 15s.

'Box toys are all German: Noah's Arks, and boxes of cavalry soldiers, and of children's skittles, and of desserts, and of railroads (all sizes, up to 20s a box), farmyards, sheepfolds, and tea-sets—in short, sets of almost anything.

'English toys are well made—such as rocking horses and large things; but in smaller things the English workmen can't pretend to vie with the Germans. The

English excel in the invention of games: round games for children, dissected puzzles, geographical and such like. The foreign articles of that kind are so slight as to be useless. What the English workmen do, they do well, solidly and enduringly—it hasn't the tinselly look of the foreign, but it's not flimsy, and is useful.

'I sell more magic lanterns and conjuring tricks than all the other houses. In such things we beat the foreigners all to nothing. Their magic lanterns are as rubbishy as ever magic was, but they're sold wonderfully low. We can't sell low to sell good—not English magic lanterns.'

Solid quality competing with the clever, the meretricious—and the lower-priced: a verdict on British industry which finds echoes still to-day.

Rocking horses

'At the door lay the torso of a rocking horse, discoloured from age, earless and legless, and battered apparently from hard usage. Near it, in startling contrast, was a newly-made horse of dazzling whiteness, placed out to dry. The interior of the workshop was crowded with timber, but on every side the staple of the place was horses, and these in all stages. Horses' trunks, heads, legs, tails and manes, of all hues and sizes, huddled on the floor, piled on the shelves, or swinging from the ceiling; horses in the rough, and horses awaiting the last polish . . .'

When Mayhew thus described the workplace of a maker of rocking horses, he was investigating a craft already a century old and a product which seems to epitomise at the same time the English love of horses and children, her imperial glories, and the finest qualities of her native craftsmanship. His informant, as always, describes the process of manufacture in detail:

'"The first process is to take a pine plank and form it, by jointing and glueing it, into a block (it used to be made out of solid timber, but the jointing is the better process). The block thus prepared is reduced by the drawing knife and the plane to the shape of the horse's body. It is then what we call bevelled and morticed, to make the holes into which the legs of the horse are placed. The head is shaped out of solid wood (pine), after a pattern cut out of strong pasteboard or thin plank, but we have merely the outline supplied by the pattern: what may be called the anatomy, with the eyes, the nostrils, teeth, and the several parts of the face, are carved out, the skill of the workman being directed altogether by his eye. The legs (of beech) are shaped without pattern, the skill of the workman again having no guide beyond his eye; and the 'tenant' is then cut in the leg—the tenant being a portion of wood left on the top of the leg to be fitted in to the mortice hole made for that end in the body. Next, the head is affixed, being jointed by a great nicety of adjustment to the body of the rocking horse, and then the toy in its rough state is complete.

'"After that it is what we call 'worked off'—that is, each part has to be duly shaped, so that all may be in accordance: head, body, legs. Without that there would be no symmetry. The 'working off' is a four hours' process (taking the average sizes), and very hard work. The first layer of composition is then applied and left to dry, which takes from eight to ten hours. The rasp is next used all over the article, and then another layer of composition is applied, and then a third: this is done to get a smooth, level surface. The last application is rubbed down with glass paper.

'"The horse is then painted, and the legs are screwed and fitted to the 'rocker', or frame, which is made before the horse is finished. It is then harnessed—we do the saddler's work ourselves; and after that the mane and tail are affixed. Then the rocking horse is complete, unless glass eyes have to be put into the head, as is often the case.

'"We divide the horses into two classes, 'gibbers' and 'racers'. A gibber seems to be inclined to gib; a racer is represented as at the very top of his speed. Gibbers have as much call as racers.

'"I cannot tell how many rocking horses may be yearly made in London. Perhaps it may be calculated this way: there are 30 men employed in making rocking horses, and each man can make two a week. That gives 3,120 a year; but as we are employed in making horses of all kinds, as well as rocking horses, you may reduce the number by one half. Yes, I think 1,500 may be about the mark."'

Some fifty years later, about the turn of the century, Joseph Lines was running a flourishing, though still modest, wooden toy manufactory in North London. His son Walter, leaving school at fourteen, began his apprenticeship in his father's rocking horse workshop, as was customary for all recruits to the firm. The horses he learned to build were made precisely as Mayhew's informant had made them. A quarter of a century on, Walter, with Triang Toys, was in charge of the largest toy factory in the world.

Meanwhile, in 1922, a young man named Ray Delfi had joined the firm of Lines Brothers. He served in it for over fifty years, and looking back over them wrote: 'I always enjoyed my work, but there was one thing that used to fascinate me, and that was our team of horse-makers. A very rough, hard-working lot they were. I have seen them drenched to the skin with sweat, carving those old horses, and still wishing I could have a go. But it was a job passed down in the family and nobody allowed in. After the war there was just one old horse-maker left, and he reluctantly showed me the way to make them.'

Ray Delfi goes on to describe the process: it is the process of 1850 still, except in the detail of the finish: 'Years ago they used to paint the horses all over with a thick coat of whitening. When this coat set, it was like a coat of plaster and of course used to cover up the faults, bad joints etc. This was then rubbed down and the spots etc added, and finally a coat of varnish. Now I use a sealer and then a couple of coats of emulsion, and then a coat of lacquer, which is of course more durable. I also found a way of using horse hair, which is more hygenic than the cows' tails which were once used. The tails used to come in large sacks from the slaughterhouse and had to be cleaned before fixing on to the horse. This was not a very pleasant task, for the smell, and then they had to be cured with allum and washed and dried—altogether a nasty job.'

When he retired, Ray Delfi thought he would make a couple of horses, 'just to amuse myself, and possibly give some child pleasure. It had to be a hobby because timber alone put the job out of reach of making anything from them.' To-day, three years later, he is still making one a month.

If wooden rocking horses have now priced themselves out of the market, there is still a demand for the skills of a Lines or a Delfi in repairing and refurbishing old ones; for these have now become treasured and valuable antiques. In her workshop by the Grand Union Canal in Camden Town, Rachel Waller

Rachel Waller repairing a rocking horse, 1976

118

maintains the same tradition of fastidious craftsmanship that Mayhew witnessed, restoring to their pristine magnificence a seemingly endless succession of rocking horses sent her from museums, stately homes, antiquaries, hospitals, and humble private citizens.

Bristol toys and white wood toys

Rocking horses were for the wealthy, of course, and were sold in shops. Wooden toys for working-class children were sold, in mid-century, chiefly from barrows and stalls in the street markets, and at fairs. They were of two broad categories: white wood toys, and greenwood or 'Bristol' toys.

'"The Bristol toys", Mayhew's informant told him, "are the common toys made for the children of the poor, and are generally retailed at a penny. They were first made in Bristol, but they have been manufactured in London for the last fifty years—though I believe there is still one maker in Bristol. Bristol toys are carts, horses, omnibuses, chaises, steamers, and such like—nearly all wheel toys. We make scratch-backs too—that has a wheel in it. These are toys used by frolicksome people, the fun consisting in suddenly 'scratching' anyone's back with the toy, which gives a sudden whirring sound.

'"To make the toys we boil the wood—green and soft, though sometimes dry; alder, willow, birch, poplar, or ash are used (white wood toys, on the other hand, were made out of deal as it came from the timber yard). When the wood has been boiled, the toy is cut with a knife and fixed together with glue, then painted."'

While wood remained the staple material for cheap toys over many decades, the trade was not immune from changes in demand reflecting developments in the real world: '"When the big horses, the spotted fellows on wheels that you must have seen, went out of fashion, it was a blow to my business. Steamers have come up rather lately; but though they have grand names painted on them: Fire Flies, and Dash Alongs, and such like, they don't go off (ie sell) as well as the old horses did. Every child has seen a horse, but there's numbers never see a steamboat, and so care nothing about them— how can they?"'

Another toymaker, however, who worked in white wood, told Mayhew that in his opinion '"fashion affects cheap toys less than any other article. This may be accounted for by the necessity of supplying them at the lowest rate, and by the anxiety of a mother who has a penny to spare causing her to buy a toy for her child such as pleased her own childhood, regardless of its want of novelty".'

Late 19th century English farm cart, *Pollock's Toy Museum*

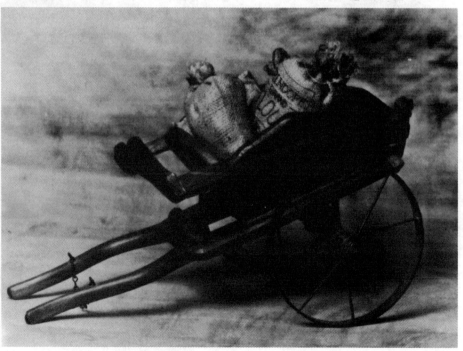

120

What worried him was the competition from foreign toys:

'"This lamb here can't be made in London for a penny, but it's brought from Germany and sold here retail at a penny. If people, even boys and girls, are paid anything abroad for making such toys, it must be next to nothing; and how they who depend on such work live at all is a puzzle to me. This foreign accordion here costs me 5s 6d a dozen wholesale (he supplied his customers with other toys, besides what he made himself); why, it couldn't be made in England for four times the price, though there's so much talk now about music. You hear, the four keys are perfect—and all for 5½ d." '

The crippled white wood toy maker

Mayhew's account of the work and circumstances of one of these white wood toy makers deserves quoting from at some length:

'On a table in the centre of the room stood a yellow pie-dish filled with a thousand springs for penny mousetraps, and behind the door was a coil of wire that twanged as it closed after me. In the little square room adjoining the parlour, and which served the poor man for both bedroom and workshop, sat the toy-maker himself, making penny mousetraps in the bed that he seldom or never quitted. On the counterpane in front was placed a small stool, and this served for his bench. He was half-dressed, having only his coat and waistcoat over his night-gown. Close within reach hung three small square bird-cages—one on one side of his bed, and two on the other—and in them frolicked his favourite goldfinches, that seemed to bear their lifelong confinement as cheerfully as their master.

'Beside the bed stood a bench littered with tools of all kinds, boxes of wire hasps, and small pieces of cut wood ready to form the sides and triggers of the mousetraps on which he was busied. The walls of the little room were hung with peepshows and toys, the hoop of an old tambourine, tiny models of ships, and wooden swords that he had made for his boy in his overtime. Over the head of the toymaker, on top of the bedstead, were a heap of patterns in paper and wood of the various articles he made, and part of the works of a new locomotive carriage to be worked by hand, which he purposed getting up for himself when he could find leisure. The works, he told me in the course of conversation, a man he had taught when a youth had promised to make for his crippled master for nothing.

Late 19th century milk float, made by J & G Lines, London, *Pollock's Toy Museum*

121

'On the stool that stood on the bed was piled a small stack of the same oblong pieces of thin deal as those on the carpenter's bench beside him, and these he was busy cutting by means of a gauge from larger pieces of the same material. His story was another of the many evidences of the sterling worth and independence of the working classes of this country.

'"I am a white wood toymaker in a small way—that is, I make a variety of cheap articles, nothing beyond a penny, in sawed and planed pine wood. I manufacture penny and halfpenny money-boxes, penny and halfpenny toy bellows, penny carts, penny garden-rollers, penny and halfpenny dolls' tables, penny wash-hand stands, chiefly for baby-houses; penny dressers, with drawers, for the same purpose; penny wheelbarrows, penny bedsteads, penny crossbows, and the penny mouse-traps, that I am about now. I make all the things that I have named for warehouses—for what are called the cheap 'Birmingham, Sheffield, and toy warehouses.'

'"I think altogether my receipts of the different masters I worked for last year came to about £120. Our income is about £1 to 22s every week, for rather more than one half of what I take goes to the expense of the material. To earn the 22s a week, you'll understand, there are four of us engaged—myself, my wife, my daughter and my son. My daughter is eighteen, and my son eleven.

'"That is my boy, sir; he's reading the *Family Friend* just now; it's a little work I take in for my girl for her future benefit: there's many useful receipts in it concerning cooking and household medicines, and good moral instruction besides. My boy goes to school every evening, and twice on a Sunday. I am willing they should find as much pleasure from reading as I have. Over and over again, when I have been in acute pain with my thigh a scientific book, or a work on history, or a volume of travels would carry my thoughts far away, and I should be happy in all my misery. I always had a love of solid works. For an hour's light reading I have often turned to works of imagination, such as Milton's *Paradise Lost* and Shakespeare's plays; but I prefer science to poetry. I think every working man ought to be acquainted with the general sciences. It gives a man a greater insight into the world and creation, and it makes his labour a pleasure and a pride to him, when he can work with his head as well as his hands.

'"I calculate that I made more than 30,000 mousetraps altogether, from January to December 1849. There are three or four other people in London making penny mousetraps besides myself. I myself brought out the penny mousetrap in its improved shape, and with the improved lever spring. I have made no calculation as to the number of mice in the country, or how soon we shall have caught them all if we go on at this rate; but I think my traps have little to do with that. They are bought more for toys than for use, though they are good for mice as well as children, let me tell you. Though we have so many dozen mousetraps about the house, I can assure you we are more troubled with mice here than most people.

'"Take one with the other, we can earn about a penny an hour; and if it wasn't for my having been a tailor originally, and applying some of my old tools to the business, we shouldn't get on as quick as we do. With my shears I can cut twenty four wires at a time, and with my thimble I thread the wires through the holes in the sides. I make the springs, cut the wires, and put them in the traps. My daughter planes the wood, gauges out the sides and bottom, bores the wire holes, and makes the doors as well. My wife nails the frames ready for wiring, and my son pulls the wires into the places after I have entered them. Then the wife springs them, after which the daughter puts in the doors, and so completes them.

'"I can't form an idea as to how many penny and halfpenny money-boxes I made last year—perhaps altogether eight thousand. I should say there must be at least 100,000 of the different sorts of cheap money-boxes manufactured in London every year.

'"I am sure, of all the toys sold, dolls and carts and horses are the greatest

122

number—the dolls are for the girls, and the carts and horses for the boys. The first toy is a doll for a girl, and a half-penny horse and a farthing whip for a boy—mind, I am speaking of poor people, who buy at the stalls in the street.

'"I was originally brought up to the tailoring business, but my master failed, and my sight kept growing weaker every year; so as I found a good deal of trouble getting employment at my own trade, I thought I would take to bird-cage making. I had been doing a little of it before, as a pastime. I was fond of birds, and fonder still of mechanics, so I was always practising my hand at some craft or other. In my overtime at the tailoring trade I used to make dissected maps and puzzles; and so, when standing for employment, I used to manage to get through the slack of the year, or while waiting orders from my master. But after I took to bird-cage making I found the employment so casual that I could not support my family at it. My children were quite young then, for I have been ten years away from my regular trade at least. This led me to turn my mind to toy making, for I found cheap toys were articles of more general sale."

'The toymaker went on to tell of the problems and anxieties of learning this new trade, in which all the family took part; and of how they had just about mastered these when he was laid up with a strumous abscess in the thigh which, besides the appalling pain, left him bedridden. "Then it was", he continued, "that my daughter, seeing the pain I suffered both in body and mind, came to me and told me not to grieve, for that she would do all the heavy work for me, and plane up the boards and cut out the work as I had done. And with the instinct of her affection—I can't call it anything else, for she learnt at once what it had taken me months to acquire—she planed and shaped the boards as well as I myself could have done it after years of practice. When you think of the difficulties she had to overcome; what a mere child she was, and had never handled a plane before; how she had the grain of the wood to find out, to learn the right handling of her tools, and many little niceties of touch that only workmen can understand—it does seem to me as if some superior power had inspired her to aid me."

'In no class', concludes Mayhew, 'have I seen such patience in sufferings, such generosity in poverty, such heroism, such charity, as I have found in the working classes of this country.'

Tops, skipping ropes, and toy guns

A toy-turner whose trade was confined to what he called 'popular' toys gave Mayhew this information:

'"The principal articles made by the toy turners in my way are humming and other tops, and skipping ropes. The humming tops are generally made of willow or alder: a block is hollowed by a tool made for the purpose, and the top is fitted to the hollowed block. We paint them ourselves, but we can't lay a picture on them, as it won't lay on account of the roundness; so the landscape, or whatever it is, is all done by a camel's-hair pencil.

'"The French have not directly affected my trade (they may indirectly), not the Germans either. It's heavy work, sir, making humming tops, and foreigners like light work best, I can tell you. Immense numbers of skipping ropes and humming tops are shipped off to America. They won't go to high-priced goods, the Yankees: the best tops and ropes are sold at home.

'"Toy-turning is all piece-work. There may be twenty men working at toy-turning in my branch; they can average 20s a week. It is a nice art: a humming top is turned according to the judgement of the workman, who must carry the pattern in his eye."'

The toy-turner's disdain for the foreigner—part chauvinism, part London pride—which colours the testimony of so many of Mayhew's informants is evident again in this statement by a maker of toy guns; only here the 'foreigner' includes Birmingham, centre of the tin-toy industry and sweat-shop of child labour:

'"I was born to the business of toy gun and pistol, as well as of tin toys, which consist of mugs and trumpets; but the foreigners have got all the trumpet trade now: what we got 30s a gross for we now only get 7s. The other tin toys, such as horses and carts, got up by machinery for a penny, are made in Birmingham. None are made in that way in London—they're but slop toys. The tin toy trade at Birmingham is the factory system with children. Think of children working hard at toys—poor little things to whom a toy is a horror!

'"In war time, bless you, that was the time for my business. There was a demand for guns then, I can tell you! I sold eight then to one that I sell now, though the population's increased so. These pistols, which I get 1s 6d a dozen for now, I had 3s 6d a dozen for then. I remember the first botched-up peace in 1802. I can just recollect the illumination. My father (I can hear him say so) thought the peace would do no good to him, but it didn't last very long, and the toy-gun trade went on steadily for years—with a bit of a fillip, now and then, after news of a victory; but the grand thing for the trade was the constant report that Bonaparte was coming—there was to be an invasion, and then every child was a soldier. Guns did 'go off' briskly at that period—anything in the shape of a gun found a customer. Working people could then buy plenty of toys for their children—and did buy them too."'

Here is another reminder that during the first half of the nineteenth century the general movement of prices was downwards: the phenomenon is sufficiently unimaginable in the second half of the twentieth to need underlining. What Mayhew's informants tend to overlook, or to conceal, is that while their earnings were indeed falling, so too—if not to the same degree—was the cost of living.

Toy drums and mechanical toys

Napoleon, apparently, did the toy drum makers no harm either. One of them revealed to Mayhew that whereas he could employ only four boys, at apprentices' wages, his uncle back in the 1800s had eleven men working for him. That was the time for the toy drum trade!

'"A best toy drum", he explained, "goes thirty-five times through our hands before it is finished, as time must be given in the working for the parts to dry and set. I and my four boys could make a gross of small wooden drums in a day, but only a dozen of the best large tin drums, highly ornamented. But we make very few tin drums now to what were made—the foreign trade have affected us so."'

The same complaint comes from a maker of 'fancy', or mechanical, toys, coupled now with a charge of plagiarism. But the English victim is a jovial fellow, and there is a broad hint that he gave as good as he got:

'"The introduction of French toys at a lower rate of duty affected my trade. I should say it has made 50% of difference to me generally. And many of the inventions or patterns that I have originated have been copied in Germany. Sometimes I got a hint from them in return for all they borrow, so to call it, from me. They rob me, and I take from them."

124

As for his product, '"My toys, though well known in the trade for their ingenuity, are not of great cost, but are chiefly within reach of the middle classes. They include animals of all descriptions: donkeys, horses, cows, cats, elephants, lions, tigers (I could make giraffes, but they're not in demand), dogs and pigs.

'"Here is a toy of my own invention. This boy is flying a kite, and you see how, by the cranks and wires, the boy appears to advance and the kite takes the air.

'"Here is a boat. These model men fix on here. By a movement I have contrived, they row the boat. The boats with the men rowing in them had as good a run as the donkeys.

'"A boy who looked in at my workshop window said, 'I'm blessed if I know what trade they are, but I heard them talk about cutting off three dozen donkeys' heads.' Donkeys' heads, you see, are made of papier maché, and the head is affixed so as to move— so are the ears, and the tail too, if demanded. I invented that donkey. The ass is made entire, and then the head is cut off to be re-fitted, with the faculty of moving . . . Here's an elephant—he moves his tail as well as his trunk.

'"If I think of inventing a new toy, I often can't sleep from thinking of it. I assure you I have often dreamed the completion of a new toy—of one that required great thought. I went to bed with the plan working in my brain, and that led to the dream."'

126

Mechanical toy, bone, of the type made by French prisoners-of-war in the time of Napoleon I *Pollock's Toy Museum*

Changes in fashion affect him too, but not necessarily adversely: '"The fashion in penny toys is very variable; but toys of twenty years back often come into fashion again. It's so with mechanical toys—moving figures. Some things I invented long ago have recently come back into fashion: the working blacksmiths and sawyers, for instance. They say that 'luck's all' in my trade, 'fancy's all'."'

A machine, in those days, was a clever contrivance, as it was to the ancient Greeks: a product of the imagination; and a mechanical toy was a toy that reflected this quality. Fancy, too, was synonymous with imagination; so a maker of mechanical toys was appropriately called a fancy toy maker. A century of progress since has given the one word the overtones of the pedestrian, the repetitive, the boring; the other, of the twee, the trivial, the meretricious.

Kites, and other fanciful toys

Mayhew's kite-maker had no hesitation in claiming for himself a 'fanciful' inventiveness:

'"I am alone in the trade", he said, "the only man in the world who makes kites after my peculiar scientific principles. This kite here, you see, folds up and will go into a case, so that you can carry it in your hand; instead of paper it is of fine cloth—fine glazed calico. By the management of the strings attached to the frame, the kite can be altered so as best to suit the wind as ascertained previous to flying, just as a sail on board ship is regulated. The tails of my kites have a series of 'cups' or 'cones', also of glazed calico. I hook them on or off, and there is no time lost.

'"The introduction of the peculiar tails of my kites trebles their sale. I have made kites twelve feet high, which have drawn a chaise holding two persons. Such kites are mostly used in drawing boats along the Rhine and other rivers: they have amazing power. A pocket handkerchief even, when held up in a wind, will be found to influence the motion of a boat.

'"We calculate that two miles is the greatest distance a kite can be made to fly, but that is only when one kite is attached to the string of another already high in the air. No one could hold a kite flown so high: a post, or something of that kind, must be used. I have made kites for carrying meat into the air to test the state of the atmosphere during the rage of the cholera.

'"I suppose there are not above twenty-five kite-makers in London. Each, I should think, may make on the average a gross of kites in a day, which is 864 a week, which is 17,280 each man for the twenty weeks the season lasts, or altogether 432,000. Average cost of the kites to the public is 4d, and my best twelve-foot kites sell at £2."'

Equally proud of his craft, and voluble too (for he was a Frenchman) was the maker of papier maché toys 'clothed' with fur or hair:

'"I can make you, if you please, the biggest animal in the world, waterproof, and that nothing can ever break, of paper or papier maché. Anything may be done with the paper, but I now use a composition as well—it is my secret of what he is made. I make only animals. I make them both way, for the ornament of the chimney and the amusement of the children. I make every domestic. There is none but I manufacture him with natural hair and wool. French poodle-dogs have the call; rabbits is good; lambs go very well; goats is middling. All the world can be supplied, from 3d up to £5, with the French poodles. I do not make the lions, nor the tigers; I make only the domestic animals, but I *could* make the lions and the tigers as well.

'"I make forty dozen domestic animals a week. The skins for the poodles and the lambs I dress myself, or they would be stink. Last year I used 4,800 lamb skins. I use nearly as many rabbit skins.

'"I do not ever admit persons into my workroom. It is a very artful ingenuity. I can beat the French—indeed, I have beat my countrymen at, for I have exportation to Paris; but the Germans come in cheap, cheap, and ruin the trade.

'"This is a barking dog. I have made him, his bark and all—you see? Yes, and you hear! The penny barks is no good—what barks can you expect for a penny? There's no get fat about him at 9d . . . This rabbit, you see, has a different skin to this other—the skin is the great cost to me. He have, too, the spring in his ears and tail, so that he lift them when the wheels go round.

'"I employ eight English women. The earnings of my women? Oh, never mind. But I am not ashamed to tell. They earn 7s; and 9s; and 11s a week, and never less than 4s. My late wife could earn twenty and two shilling a week in this trade, but then she had the talent. Oh no, none can now earn like that: they have not the art in it, the nature, the interest."'

A woman artisan had applied her imaginative talents to softball making:

'"I make only the better sort. Here is one, made of different coloured cloths, you perceive, in diamonds of different lengths and widths. The joinings are covered over with this light gilt wire. That toy, sir, is my own invention, I might say. I invented it with six quarterings, and it has thirty-six. I make such like in velvet. They are really beautiful. They're stuffed with the softest and finest seal's hair: so soft, the best hair is, that with a child's strength it wouldn't break a window, unless it was very bad glass, even if flung right against it. They're drawing room balls. I work, sir, sometimes, for the Royal Family. The order comes to me through a warehouse, but I supply the article direct.

'"These balls here, you see, are coloured leathers, without gilt wire, but well made. Each diamond is cut out according to a nice iron pattern . . . These are common things which I'm forced to make for the low shops. They won't wear.'''

Even the toy basket maker, whose room Mayhew found very poorly furnished, and where all told of 'a dreary poverty', yet had the pride of one who had done his own thing and who was, in his own way, unique:

'''I myself am the only man in all the world who makes the penny pincushion-baskets. It's just a pincushion in a little basket, but I started it. I sell it for a penny now with the cushion. Sixteen years ago I could sell more, oh, that I could, a great deal more, and the same size, without the cushions than I now can sell with them. But in that time a penny article of a nicer sort was a rarity, and so it went off (sold well). But now there's penny books, and penny papers, and penny numbers, and penny everythings, and nothing's so scarce that way as the pennies themselves. In the last season I only got 1s 9d clear profit on six dozen, or 10s 6d a week. It's an awful trade.'''

Finally, an aristocrat among the artisans of the toy trade, though distinguished for his intelligence and craftsmanship rather than for inventive flair: the camera obscura maker.

'''I have known the camera obscura business for 25 years or so, but I can turn my hand to clock-making, or anything. My father was an optician, employing many men; but the introduction of steam machinery has materially affected the optical glass grinder—which was my trade at first. In a steam-mill in Sheffield, one man and two boys can now do the work that kept sixty men going.

'''The only improvement I can remember in the making of the cameras is this: Formerly the object-glass was a fixture in the wood of the box and could only take an object at a certain distance; whereas by applying a movable brass tube, with the glass in it, you can command objects at any distance, adjusting it

Scene from *Goody Goose*, JK Green, 1842

129

precisely on the principle of a telescope. Too much light obliterates your object, and too little light won't define it. Here is the stuff of the box body, cedar—all blacked on the inside, so as to exclude any false light. The bottom is deal, and the natural colour of that or of the cedar would obliterate an object by giving false lights.

'"In making my cameras I test them from this door to objects at a distance. It gives every line of those tiles, every shape of those chimney-pots, and every tumble of those tumbler pigeons. So I detect any error in the focus, and regulate it. I must test them at a good height, with a good light. A fog gives you only a fog—no defined object. The perfect adjustment of the focus, and indeed of every portion, is the nice art of my trade."'

Crackers

'His parlour', wrote Mayhew, 'as well as the window of his workshop, presented an admixture sufficiently curious. Old foreign paintings— religious, mythological, or incomprehensible—were in close connection with unmistakeable Hogarth prints. Barometers (for these were also "made and repaired") showed that it was "set fair", and alongside them were grosses of detonating crackers. Of frames and mouldings there was a profusion, and in all stages, from the first rough outline to the polished gilding'. It seems altogether appropriate that the cracker-maker should have been an Italian, and moreover endowed with a versatility, as his surroundings testify, worthy of a fellow-countryman of Leonardo. Mayhew's rendering of the Italian's rendering of the English language adds a further layer of picturesqueness to his narrative:

'"Yes. I make de detonating crackers, and am de only man in England skilful to make dem. It is a grand secret, mine art. It live in my breast alone—de full, entire secret. I will show you de pulling crackers. Dey go in wid de pastry-cook's tings at de parties of de rich. A gentleman say to a lady, so I have heard, in de pleasantness od de party, 'Please to pull'. Yes, indeed, as dey write above de bells. And so de pretty lady pull, and de cracker goes bang, and de lady goes 'Ah-h-h!' quite sudden too, of course, dough she must have known before dat de crack was to come. Ah, sir, dey seldom tink of de Italian artist who make de pulling cracker dat has brought out her nice 'Ah-h-h!' for 3½d de gross—dat is all we get for de dozen dozen. I dare say de rich fashionable pastrycook get a great deal for dem, I don't know how much; dey are sold at de retail shops, dat are not high shops, at a halfpenny a dozen.

'"Den de detonatings—dem wot are trone down on de stones, and go bang, and make de people passing go start. Do dey cause many accidents, do I tink? Bah, nonsense. It is de play of de boys: it keep dem out of mischief.

'"All last year I sold, as near as I can tell, 50 gross of de pulling, and 50 of de detonating. Dat is—yes, no doubt—14,480 a week, or 748,800 a year. How curious! More than seven hundred dousand bang-bangs made in dis little place! Dere is danger, perhaps, in de make to some, but no to de right artist."'

Magic lanterns

Most of the toys Mayhew's informants describe show little change from one decade to the next. Not so the magic lantern, which in the hands of clever artisans reflects a story of continuous development:

'"I have known the business of magic lantern making thirty-five years. It was then no better than the common galantee shows in the streets, Punch and Judy, or any peepshow. There was no science and no art about it: just grotesque things for children, as 'Pull devil and pull baker'." He showed me one in which a cat was busy at the washtub, with handkerchiefs hanging on her tail to dry; Judy, with a glass in her hand, was in company with a nondescript sort of devil, smoking a pipe; and a horse was driving a man, who carried the horse's panniers.

'"There were also things called 'comic changes' in vogue at that period. As the glasses moved backward and forward, fitted into a small frame like that of a boy's slate, a beggar was shown as if taking his hat off, and Jim Crow turning about

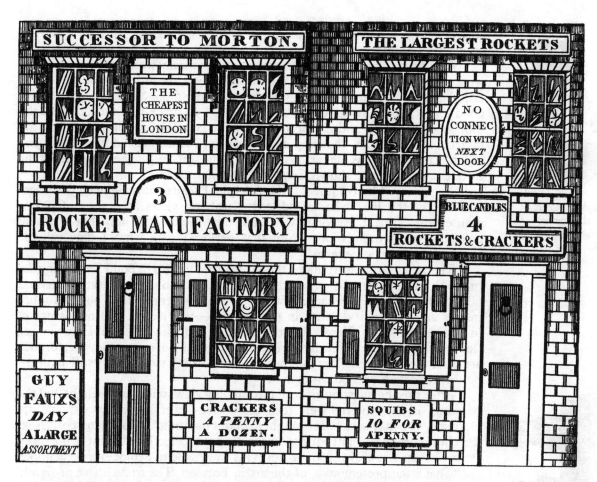

West's Phantasmagoria Magic Lantern and Optical Diagonal Machine for viewing Pictures. From *The Boy's Book of Amusement*, late 19th century

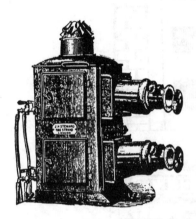

Bi-Unial Lantern, late 19th century

Spectre Magic Lantern, from *The Boy's Book of Amusement*

and wheeling about, and a blacksmith hammering. There were no theatrical scenes beyond Harlequins and clowns.

'"About thirty years ago the diagrams for astronomy were introduced. These were made to show the eclipses of the sun and moon, the different constellations, the planets with their satellites, the phases of the moon, and the comets with good long tails. Next came moving diagrams—so made that they showed the motion of the earth and its rotundity, by the course of a ship painted on the lantern; and the tides, the neap and the spring, as influenced by the sun and moon. Then there was the earth going round the sun, and as she passed along the different phases were shown, day here and night there.

'"Mr Henry, who conjured at the Adelphi Theatre some eighteen years ago, was one of the first who introduced dissolving views at a place of public amusement. Then, these views were shown by the oil light only, but even that created a great impression. From that period I date what I may call the popularity of magic lanterns.

'"Then the Careys introduced the gas microscope, up in Bond Street—on the principle of the magic lantern, only better glazed, showing the water lions and other things in a drop of stagnant water. Thames water may do. I now introduce insects and butterflies' wings in my lanterns—real insects and real wings of insects on the slides. Here's the sting, tongue and wing of a bee. Here you see flowers. Those leaves of the fern are really beautiful—of course they are, for they are from the fern itself. You can magnify them to any size, and it's still nature—no disproportion and no distortion.

'"After this the question arose of introducing views with the limelight, but the paintings in the lanterns were then too coarse—every defect was shown up, glaringly, you may say. That brought in better paintings—at a greater cost. Next the chromatrope was introduced—revolving stars chiefly, the hint being taken from Chinese fireworks. Mount Vesuvius was made to explode, and such like.

'"That's the present state of the art in London. The trade is five or sixfold what I once knew it. Landscapes, Fingal's Caves, cathedrals, sea views are most popular now. In the landscapes we give the changes from summer to winter—from a bright sun in July to the snow seen actually falling in January.

'"I make between 500 and 600 a year: I think I make one half of those made. The lowest price of a well-made lantern is 7s 6d, and so on up to £20 for dissolving and double lanterns.'"

Copper and pewter toys

Here, by contrast, is the skilled worker in a traditional material: copper.

'"I think I can earn 20s a week, if my wife and I work early and late, which we do when we've call: sometimes we earn only 10s. I think I could do well in New York, where my trade in not known at all. It was very good once, but now it's come down very bad in this country, and I should like to try another. People here haven't got money for toys; besides, mine last too long, they ought to break quicker.'" Yet this same man could declare, '"I make all that are made in London—yes, in the world. Here's the world's shop, sir, this little place, for copper toys!'" He describes his work thus:

'"At present I make chiefly copper tea-kettles, coffee-pots, coal-scuttles, warming pans, and brass scales. These are the most run on, but I make besides brass and copper hammers, saucepans, fish kettles, stewpans and other things.

'"There are sixteen pieces in one copper tea-kettle: first the handle, which has three pieces, seven pieces in the top and cover (lid), one piece for the side, two in the spout, one for the bottom, and two rivets to fix the handle—in all, sixteen.

'"Copper toys are the hardest of any toy work, I consider. The copper, you see, must be 'planished', that is, polished by hammering it with a steel-faced 'head', four inches square. All the kettles, pots and pans I make are fit to boil water in, cook anything you like in—every one of them. You can make broth in them. They are made on exactly the same principles as the large kettles, except that those are brazed together, and mine are soft-soldered.'"

132

As painstaking in his craft, and even worse provided for, was Mayhew's pewter toy maker, who had 'the pale and subdued look which I have often seen in mechanics whose earnings are limited and uncertain. "I make", he said, "only sets of tea services, such as these I show you, sir, which consist of twenty-three pieces: six cups, six saucers, six spoons, sugar-tongs, milk-pot, tea-pot and lid, and sugar basin. I can make three dozen sets in a day—that is 828 pieces, and would require ten hours' good work. Each piece is cast in a mould, and I will show you how.

'"Here I sit before the fire, with the melted pewter in this pan on the fire before me. I hold the mould in my hand, and dip my ladle into the melted pewter, and fill the mould with it. The mould, of course, is different for each piece. I often scald my fingers and hands—here is an old burn, and here another. I mix my own pewter: tin, and lead, and spelter. The spelter is to give it a colour. The commonest pewter would not answer my purpose.

'"The mould is all brass, and when filled with the metal is at once dipped into water to cool; then the metal is turned out, and it has to be pared and trimmed ready for use afterwards. To make one set by itself would take me two full hours. You may cast a number before you even get the right heat. As it is, I cast one lot by itself—go on casting teapots, and then any of the other parts of the service. As fast as they are cast, I apply this knife as if opening an oyster, and open the mould, and out comes the article.

'"Last year I made, one week with another, six dozen sets a week; or 3,744 sets, that is 86,112 pieces, in the year. There is another man in the trade who, with the help of the eight men he has, can make three gross of tea or dinner services in a day. He makes largely for shipping—to America and Ireland principally, where I've heard they're not up to toy-making."'

Our informant works out this man's annual output, adds in that of a third worker, and tots up the total to something more than half a million pieces annually. Indefatigably, he goes on: '"I reckon there are twice as many (in pieces) made of the other pewter toys, such as gridirons, fire sets, kitchen sets, carts, horses, omnibuses, steam-engines, soldiers, sailors, drummers, milkmaids, cats and kittens, dogs with baskets in their mouths, shepherds and shepherdesses, and some more"'; and triumphantly produces his final figure of 1,102,298 pieces a year '"in my trade in London, shepherdesses and all included".' Arithmetical precision, for him as for so many of his fellow artisans, matches precision in craftsmanship.

Mademoiselle Proche in the opera *Un Jour à Naples*. One of Queen Victoria's dolls, in a yellow silk frock with brown velvet trimmings

Toy theatres: William West

The nineteenth century acquired a new audience for the theatre: the industrial proletariat. The theatre responded by providing vamped-up Shakespeare, exotic melodrama, extravagant spectacle, and pantomime. Its history is recorded in the 'penny plain, twopence coloured' sheets of the toy theatre which by Mayhew's time were being turned out by dozens of jobbing printers plying little cottage industries in the back streets of Covent Garden. The doyen of them all, William West, was an old man, and quite a celebrated one, when Mayhew came to visit him.

'"I am a maker of children's theatres, and a theatrical print publisher"', West told him. '"I have been in the line ever since 1811. I was originally in the circulating library and haberdashery line. We had a glass case of toys as well, and among the toys we sold children's halfpenny lottery prints—common things that were done in those days, sir. Well, you see, my parents used to be at Covent Garden Theatre, and I took it in my head to have a print done of Mother Goose. I can show you the old original print. You shall see, sir, the first theatrical print ever published.

'"I brought out one a day for three years. The print consisted of eight characters in as many separate compartments. The first was the elder Grimaldi as Clown, the second Bologna as Harlequin, the third was the Columbine of that day— oh dear, what was her name? The other compartments were filled with other characters in the piece.

'"I brought out this print, you'll understand, to please the children. And so it did—went like wildfire among the young folks. Shopkeepers came to me from far and near for 'em. Bad as the drawing of these here is, I can assure you it was a great advance on the children's halfpenny lotteries.

'"At first we didn't do any but the principal characters in a piece. After that we was asked by the customers for theayters to put the characters in, so I got up the print of a stage front, thinking that the customers would get the woodwork done themselves. But after the stage front they wanted the theayters themselves of me more than ever, so I got some made; and then the demand got so great that I was obliged to keep three carpenters to make 'em for me. Afterwards I was hobligated to make scenery and to do the sets of characters complete.

'"I used to make, I think, about fifty toy theayters a week. Some theaytres I made came to as much as £20 apiece. They was fitted up with very handsome fronts—generally 'liptic arch fronts, built all out of wood, with ornaments all over it—and they had machinery to move the side wings on and off; lamps in front, to rise and fall with machinery, and side lamps to turn on and off to darken the stage, and trick sliders to work the characters on and change the pantomime tricks; then there was machinery to make the borders rise and fall as well, and cut traps to open for the scenery to go up and down through the stage.

'"*The Miller and his Men* has sold better than any other play I ever published. I wore out a whole set of copper plates of that there. It's the last scene, with the grand explosion of the mill, as pleases the young 'uns, uncommon. Some on 'em greases the last scene with butter—that gives a werry good effect with a light behind; but varnish is best, I can't bear butter. Some of them explosions we has made in wood work, and so arranged that the mill can fly to pieces: they come out to about 4s 6d. apiece.

'"The next most taking play out of my shop has been *Bluebeard.* That the boys like for the purcession over the mountains, a-coming to take Fatima away; and then there's the blue chamber with the skellingtons in it—that's werry good too, and has an uncommon pretty effect with a little blue fire, though it, in general, sets all the audience a-sneezing.

'"Here I've got handy the first likeness I ever did; and I should like you to see it, and have it all correct, 'cause you see it's a matter of history, like. Here's all my large portraits—there's 111 of them. This here's one of Liston as Moll Flagon; and that's Mr H Johnson as Glassier: I think the part was in a tragedy called *The Hillusion.* That was the werry first portrait as I published.

From a sheet of tricks in Webb's *Harlequin Dame Trump*

134

Robert Louis Stevenson and
Winston Churchill, two toy theatre
devotees

Grand evening rehearsal of *The
Miller and his Men*, from *Young
Troublesome*, designed and etched
by John Leech

'"The portraits I have just been showing you are 2d plain, 4d coloured—but they don't sell now; the penny has quite knocked them up. Then there's other people wot makes as low as a halfpenny, but they ain't like the performance at all. You see the cheap shops makes up the dresses with silk, and tinsel, and foil, but I never did. My customers used to do some, but to my mind it spoilt the figures, and took away all the good drawing from them."

'I remarked that he had printed a great many portraits of Mr Bradley. He said that gentleman was such a great favourite with the children: he made himself up so murderous looking, and then he was such a fine swordsman with TP Cooke, you'ld think they were going to kill one another. It was quite beautiful to see 'em—people used to go on purpose. He told me he had printed more portraits of Huntley, Bradley and Blanchard than of any other members of the theatrical profession—with the exception of Kean in *Richard III*.

In West's world too, alas, nothing is quite what it once was. He was not to know that 125 years later the bawdy song sheets he used to sell on the quiet would reappear in a handsome, glossy volume; nor that the editor of this volume would still be performing *The Miller and his Men* to enraptured, and participating, audiences of children and adults; nor that *Bluebeard* would be produced in Pollock's Toy Museum to mark the centenary of Benjamin Pollock's accession to the little shop in Hoxton which came to symbolise the indestructability of the toy theatre.

Among all the famous men—Charles Dickens, Robert Louis Stevenson, GK Chesterton and others—who spent long, happy hours of childhood playing toy theatre, there were few who did not have, like William West, a particular affection for *The Miller and his Men*. Certainly it was the favourite also of Sir Winston Churchill, another toy theatre enthusiast: Mr George Speaight, the toy theatre's historian, traces its influence as a school of rhetoric in Sir Winston's famous speech in the House of Commons in June, 1940:

'We shall not flag or fail . . . We shall defend our island, whatever the cost may be. We shall fight on the beaches, we shall fight on the landing grounds, we shall fight in the streets, we shall fight in the hills. We shall never surrender.'

Is there not, asks George Speaight, a remembered echo here of the miller Grindoff, pursued by Count Fribourg and his German soldiery, making a last stand on the gallery of his mill?

'Surrender!' cries the Count.

'Never!' replies the Miller. 'Surrender? Foolhardy slave, I have sworn never to descend from this spot alive unless with liberty!'

Count Wretch! Your escape is now impossible. Surrender!

Miller Never.

The gunpowder train is fired. The mill explodes in a final uproar and conflagration.

Grindoff, *The Miller & his Men*, JK Green, 1840

Banditti Carousing *The Miller & his Men*

137

Toy soldiers: William Britain

Whatever influence the toy theatre may have had on Churchill's magnificent command of the English language, it was certainly the long hours he spent manoeuvring his armies of tin soldiers which resulted in his being sent as a cadet to the Royal Military College, Sandhurst. As he records in *My Early Life*:

'My military career was entirely due to my collection of soldiers. I had ultimately nearly 1,500. The day came when my father himself paid a formal visit of inspection. All the troops were arranged in the correct formation of attack. He spent twenty minutes studying the scene ... At the end he asked me if I would like to go into the Army. I thought it would be splendid to command an army. I said "Yes" at once.

'For years I thought my father, with his experience and flair, had discerned in me the qualities of military genius. But I was told later that he had only come to the conclusion that I was not clever enough to go to the Bar.'

Churchill's toy soldiers were probably—whisper it!—German-made; but soon a native army, providentially named Britain's, was to rout them. For in 1860 William Britain had brought his family from Birmingham to London and set them up in the metal toy making business.

Here they set out to manufacture metal toys that moved—by a simple clockwork mechanism, or through a flywheel set in motion by pulling a string, or by fine sand trickling through holes and setting some cogs turning. They produced walking bears and performing poodles, Chinese mandarins drinking tea and Highlanders emptying bottles of whisky, equestriennes performing on horseback and Indian jugglers coaxing snakes out of baskets.

By the 1890s, however, they had given up the manufacture of these amusing, but expensive, toys to concentrate entirely on soldiers. The ingenious elder son, William, developed and perfected the hollow cast method of moulding metal—an important new process because it was quicker in production and, since it used less metal than solid casting, also cheaper. It thus enabled Britain to compete with the virtual German monopoly in this field.

The prime difficulty for Britain's was to combat reluctance within the home toy trade, which was geared to acceptance of German supplies. Eventually, however, Gamage's agreed to provide a shop window, and the first set of soldiers—Life Guards—was put on sale. Later, Gamage's were to devote a whole department to Britain's models; and within a few years of breaking into the German market Britain's were actually exporting model soldiers to Germany.

New series of soldiers were constantly brought out. Following the Life Guards came the Highland regiments: the Black Watch, the Argylls, the

Toy soldiers from Britain's catalogue, 1935

Facing: The Worcestershire Regiment 29th and 13th foot soldiers, manufactured by Britain c. 1910

The Brigade of Foot Guards.
The Grenadiers. The Coldstreams. The Scots Guards.
The Irish Guards.   The Welsh Guards.

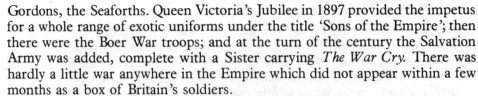

Gordons, the Seaforths. Queen Victoria's Jubilee in 1897 provided the impetus for a whole range of exotic uniforms under the title 'Sons of the Empire'; then there were the Boer War troops; and at the turn of the century the Salvation Army was added, complete with a Sister carrying *The War Cry*. There was hardly a little war anywhere in the Empire which did not appear within a few months as a box of Britain's soldiers.

Britain's success was due to no mere patriotic preference by customers wanting 'British toys for British boys': their models were an improvement on the Germans'. Hollow casting meant that figures were moulded in the round, and therefore superior to the traditional 'flattie' type; moreover their uniforms were more accurate, and they were made to particular scales—an infallible attraction for schoolboys. The Germans had no set scale, and frequently included different sizes in the same box: this mattered little to small children, but to the pocket-money age-group with the collecting urge realism and accuracy are very important.

During the Great War Britain's managed to keep going until 1917, when the factory was taken over for munitions. Afterwards, although soldiers never fell out of favour among children, war-weary parents tended to prefer pastoral toys, and many stopped buying military ones.

Britain's responded by producing The Model Home Farm (1924), which had the advantage of appealing to girls as well as boys. The first dozen or so models— farmers, cows, horses and so on— were soon followed by an almost unending stream of additions and accessories, enough to satisfy even the most acquisitive child. The rarest item is supposed to be the Village Idiot—added to the catalogue after Queen Mary, on being shown a large layout of Britain's Home Farm at the British Industries Fair, is said to have exclaimed, 'But surely the village idiot is missing?'

Through the 1920s products became much more diverse: zoo, miniature garden and circus followed hard on the farm—all in the same style, and with scores of pieces to be bought one by one. Then came motor vehicles and aeroplanes; and by the eve of the Second World War the thick catalogue boasted railway accessories, hunting scenes, scouts and guides, Christmas cake novelties, flower arrangement supports, diminutive garden gnomes, Snow White and the Seven Dwarfs, and Mickey Mouse. A Coronation Coach was produced in 1936 for the accession of Edward VIII, but when he abdicated Britain's had quickly to withdraw the stocks and add another figure—to represent King George VI and Queen Elizabeth. Britain's are said to have offered to replace with the new model any coach that had already been bought with only one figure in it.

Britain's success bred imitators. As early as 1903 there were four court cases for piracy, which they fought with some success; but the new sculpture copyright law of 1911 failed to cover model soldiers, and there were subsequently many copyists, the most blatant being the firm of John Hill & Co, later Johillco. This firm was established by a Mr Wood, who in 1900 had been one of Britain's employees. He imitated nearly all Britain's ranges, including the farm and station people and accessories and the dolls' house utensils, and many of his copies are quite indistinguishable from Britain's originals.

After World War I Britain's adopted plastics. Their initial series of miniatures, Herald, was created by Mr Zang in 1957: a year later plastic was extended to the farm series. Lead, at least for the home market, was discontinued in the 1960s.

A pugnacious pacifist: HG Wells

HG Wells was another toy soldier addict. It was an addiction which outlasted childhood and which, like other enthusiasms, he harnessed to propagate a passionately held Cause. Here is his friend Charles Masterman's description of the Wells sitting-room:

'The floor was converted by toy bricks and impedimenta into a wild, rocky scene. The instruments were the ordinary large tin soldiers and the extraordinary, accurately shooting, little brass cannon. The game's charm lay in the combination of actual skill in shooting with the planning of cunning device in strategy and tactic. Moves were limited by time on each side, and everything depended on rapidity. So that I have seen harmless guests, entering for tea, greeted ferociously with the injunction "Sit down and keep your mouth shut!". . . A game which began at 10.00 and ended only at 7.30, in which Wells had illegitimately pressed non-combatants into his army—firemen, cooks, shopkeepers and the like—, and in which a magnificent shot from the other end of the floor destroyed a missionary fleeing on a dromedary—the last representative of the nation which had marched so gaily into battle so many hours before.'

And here is Wells himself, in his book *Floor Games*, published prophetically enough on the eve of the First World War, enlisting these very military exercises in the cause of pacifism:

'Let us put this prancing monarch and that silly scaremonger, these excitable "patriots" and those adventurers, and all the practitioners of Weltpolitik into one vast Temple of War, with cork carpets everywhere, and plenty of little trees and little houses to knock down, and cities and fortresses, and unlimited soldiers—tons, cellars-full—and let them lead their own lives away from us.

'Here is war down to rational proportions, and yet out of the way of mankind . . . For my part, I am prepared. I have nearly 500 men, more than a score of guns, and I twirl my moustache and hurl defiance eastward from my home in Essex. And not only eastward.

'I would conclude this little discussion with one other disconcerting and

141

exasperating sentence for the admirers and practitioners of Big War. I have never yet met in little battle any military gentleman, any captain, major, colonel, general, or eminent commander, who did not presently get into difficulties and confusions among even the elementary rules of the battle. You have only to play out little wars three or four times to realise just what a blundering thing Big War must be.'

The nursery world

Most young children, before the 19th century, toiled the day long as their parents did: outdoors, working in the fields or minding animals; indoors, in dingy rooms, endlessly weaving, sewing, cutting, hammering, to help make by hand the small necessities of life. Then, as factories replaced handwork, child labour—in towns at least—became dispensable. But it was cheap; so it survived, whittled down by successive Acts of Parliament, till in the 1870s compulsory education brought a kind of liberation to the under-twelves: the company of their peers in safe, disciplined conditions; space and time, exiguous but welcome, for games traditional or invented in the school playground.

For an increasing number of children there was, by now, far more than this. Industrialisation had brought a rapid increase in national wealth, and a rapid expansion of the mercantile and professional middle class which fostered this wealth and was its chief beneficiary. More and more parents could afford to bring up their children in a protected and privileged world; so nannies, then governesses, were engaged to take charge of their nursery years, while boarding schools in the country, liberally equipped with playing fields, supplied the training thought appropriate for boy- or girlhood and adolescence.

The school day was filled with class or team activities. The nursery day, while it included instruction in the three Rs and in useful jobs like sewing, still left many hours to be filled, especially in wet weather, by harmless and if possible improving pastimes. So from the mid-century on there was an ever-growing demand for indoor games and toys: it was met by new firms some of which are still household words to-day. John Jacques, for instance, published his *County Cards of England* in 1850, followed ten years later by *Happy Families,* designed by Tenniel, the original illustrator of *Alice in Wonderland.* Word-Making, Halma, Spoof and many other board games were brought out by Chad Valley in the 80s and 90s. Dolls' houses, by now, were no longer Baby Houses made for the daughter of the family by craftsmen on some ducal estate: they were manufactured in batches and could be bought in any good toyshop. So could the new dappled horses on safety rockers, invented in the USA in 1880. Machine-made paper, together with photogravure and other new printing processes, meanwhile brought into the nursery brightly-coloured scraps for sticking into special albums, a wealth of cheap cardboard and paper toys, and above all a whole new range of books specially written and illustrated for children.

Children, in fact, had at last acquired a distinctive identity; they were recognised as having distinctive needs; and a distinctive market set out to cater for them. They had some decades yet to wait for the more questionable blessings of child-centred education, children's rights, and children's charters: meanwhile they —the middle class ones at least—had Henty, and Ballantyne, and Kate Greenaway; they had the *Boys Own* and *Girls' Own Papers;* they had Noah's Arks and boxes of bricks and jigsaws and rocking horses. And they had their nannies.

Some were blest with the type of nanny of whom Joyce Grenfell was later to write: 'She may not have had many books, but she was wise, steady and to be relied on for the unchanging certainty of selfless love. I now realise my nanny was a socialist as well as a royalist and a nonconformist. She also had a slightly shamefaced faith in what the tea-leaves revealed. Above all she was good as gold, strong and gentle.'

But for others the early years could still be austere, the nursery a place making few concessions to child. Here is a passage from Margaret Lane's biography of Beatrix Potter:

Late 19th century dolls' house,
Pollock's Toy Museum

Below: Toy butcher's shop, late
19th century, *John Judkin Memorial
Collection*

'She was provided with a Scottish nurse of Calvinistic principles; she had a clean starched piqué frock every morning and "cotton stockings striped round and round like a zebra's legs"; a cutlet and rice pudding came up the back stairs every day for lunch; and in the afternoon, unless it rained, McKenzie the nurse took her for a good walk. What more could a child want? Nothing, perhaps; for quiet, solitary and observant children create their own world and live in it, nourishing their imaginations on the material at hand; and she was not at all unhappy. Did not Ruskin, as a child, have as his sole plaything a bunch of keys? The child Beatrix Potter had more, much more; she had a "dilapidated black wooden doll called Topsy and a very grimy, hard-stuffed, once-white flanellette pig", which did not belong to her, but which was brought out on special occasions from the bottom drawer of her grandmother's secretaire; and the house contained the Waverley Novels, on which she learned to read, and the complete works of Miss Maria Edgeworth; and she composed hymns and "sentimental ballad descriptions of Scottish scenery", and in her unmolested upper story constructed a child's defence against the airless grown-up life which went on below.'

An exceptional child, perhaps, to find in the very austerity of her circumstances the spur to explore the inner world of her imagination—the exception to prove the Victorian discovery that children deserve to be treated as children. Margaret Lane's own strong hint that children can also be wiser than their parents is a post-Victorian concept, but inconceivable until the Victorians had established the unique character of childhood.

'Milly' in the nursery

'Milly' was Eleanor Acland's pet name as a child: she used it when she wrote, fifty years later, about her childhood in the 80s. Nowhere is the atmosphere of a late-Victorian nursery more lovingly evoked. Pride of place goes to the rocking horse:

'In our small world within the great all of things, the inhabitants closest to ourselves were our playthings and toys. The King of them was Dapple-Grey,

Pricking and sewing card worked by a small child, 1900

145

Victorian scraps re-printed by
Mamelok Press, Bury St Edmunds

Right: Milly, drawn in colour from
an old photograph by Frank
Stanley, c 1888

FATE LADY.

From *The Girl's Own Toy Maker,*
(also with accompanying
instructions), 1863

the rocking horse. His galloping form straddled across the dining-room window.
For us children he was playmate rather than plaything. George used to say of
him, as Father said of his hunters: "Nonsense! Not an ounce of vice in him. Just
his play!" But admittedly he was of a high spirit. You could tell as much, even
before you mounted on to his back or his rockers, by the bold wild stare of his
eye, by his scarlet, distended nostrils, the proud curve of his neck. Betty, whose
roundabout figure did not lend itself to rocking-horsemanship, sat snug on the
saddle—the place of minimum motion; Milly and George sat (or in moments of
the greatest daring, stood) on either end of Dapple's green rockers, one grasping
his head and the other his tail. And oh, what a breathtaking alternation it was, at
one moment to behold Dapple's, Betty's, and George's heads, one beyond
another, towering above you, George's almost ceiling high, and the next to be
flung with a lurch away up and up till you saw George far below you, almost on
his back on the carpet.'

146

The dolls' house too looms large in Milly's memory, for it was indeed substantial; but was it, she seems to ask, really very well adapted to the needs of three boisterous children?

'It had eight rooms on three stories: downstairs, on the left, was the kitchen, on the right the dining-room, with the staircase hall in between; upstairs, two bedrooms and a room which we sometimes used as the nursery, sometimes as the drawing-room; and above these again, two attics. This mansion always seemed to promise a good spell of play. One of us would say: "Hurrah, it's a real wet day. Let's play the whole morning with the dolls' house." There had to be a definite decision, because the windowed front of the house was kept locked, and a grown-up had to come and unlock it and latch it back against the wall and tell us to mind and not go breaking the glass. Then, somehow, when we had straightened up the fallen bits of furniture, and tidied the beds, and had a roll-call of the doll inhabitants, we generally failed to develop any really amusing game. There stood the eight rooms, three-walled like those on a theatre stage; but whether we set out to produce the tragedy of how all the dolls' house children died of the measles, or the comedy of how Nurse fell into the bath, the drama would hang fire. The doll actors, moved by our Brobdingnagian hands thrust in, often at cross purposes, from the auditorium, failed to play their roles at all convincingly; they were of flagrantly ill-assorted sizes, the baby of the family being much larger than the mother, and they had a way of flopping limply over the furniture at tense moments.'

Then, rag dolls for punishment, wax for admiration—and tragedy:

'There was Captain Mawley, who
        Was so pawley,
Captain Mawley went to bed.
Captain Mawley got more pawley,
In the morning he was dead.

He was the wag of the doll world, a flabby rag doll in a tattered knitted suit, whom we had inherited from a former generation. When we built a high tower of bricks, he always had to sit on the floor inside it, and while we flung brick after brick at the tower, we sang the above jingle, repeating the words "in the morning" over and over again, so that the word "dead", bawled with the full force of our lungs, coincided with the final crash and totter of the tower.

From *The Girl's Own Paper*, 1894
Instructions for making the rag doll accompanied her picture

Left: Illustration to Mary Russell Mitford's story, *The Two Dolls* 1864

147

'The other special doll was Lady Fair. Captain Mawley was common property, but Lady Fair was Milly's very own; no one else might play with her. The devotion that Milly felt for her was a jealous passion, three parts pride to one of affection. Milly adored the very name she had invented for her beloved. No other little girl had ever had a doll called Lady Fair; nor, so far as Milly knew, a doll with hazel-brown eyes instead of the usual China blue.

'But it fell on a blazing midsummer day that when we were summoned indoors for our mid-day rest and nursery dinner, we left our company of toys lying out on the rug under the shade of the chestnut tree where we had spent the morning in play. Two hours or so later we ran out again. The shadow of the tree had shifted eastward, and the strew of toys, including Lady Fair, lay in the full blaze of the sun. As Milly stooped to pick up Lady Fair, she recoiled in horror. Lady Fair's cheeks, that had been "so red and so white, dears", had turned a murky cream colour, her nose had melted into her cheeks, and her eyelids were permanently gummed down over those bewitching hazel eyes.

'"The sun's been and melted her," said George. "Now she's your poor blind Lady Fair."

'Here was the occasion for Milly to take into her arms the doll that still for old sake's sake should have been the prettiest doll in the world. But somehow it wasn't like that at all. No spring of pity for her beloved welled up in Milly's heart, nothing but repugnance as vehement as her former love had been.

'"Ugh! She's horrid. Beastly! She's not my Lady Fair any more," she cried. Shuddering, she seized the doll by the skirts and bore her indoors, head downwards, to the nursery. There, without another glance at her ruined beauty, she crammed her into the darkest corner of the toy cupboard.'

Wise before their time, Milly and Co anticipated the educational pundits of the next generation in deciding there was nothing quite like bricks for adaptability:

'The part that dolls were intended by our betters to play in our games was actually taken by individual bricks out of the big brick-box. In their proper character of building material these bricks were most satisfactory. We built them into houses and stables, forts and bridges, but most often into one chimney-like tower, so high that we had to stand on a chair to finish the narrowed top-layers. We stood them up on end at other times, two inches or so apart, in a circle round the nursery table, and then with a flip of the finger knocked one over, and watched the consequent succession of falls pass like magic from one brick to another till they all lay prone.

'But certain ones of these bricks served us in another capacity. To everyone but ourselves the whole two hundred or so looked exactly alike, just uniform wooden blocks about five inches long and an inch or two thick. To our minds there were some dozen of them that had distinct personalities. There was, for instance, Princess Lily, distinguished by her wavy hair—a pale ripple in the grain; Sarah, the bad girl, who was a shade darker than any of the others; Herbert, the tell-tale, with a hole, like a mouth, where a knot had been; General Gordon, who wore a sword or a mark that stood for a sword; Bill, the pirate, with a black patch over one eye. I forget the rest. But there were enough of these special bricks to "be" all the people we needed for christenings, weddings, shipwrecks, burglaries, or whatever play we wanted to produce. They acted their parts much better than any dolls, for they did not circumscribe our imaginations by staring at us with smugly pretty faces; and having no arms nor legs they could not ruin a performance by assuming, as the dolls did, unsuitable attitudes at critical turns in the drama.'

And the Victorian Sunday? It was not, for Milly, the lack-lustre day of atonement depicted in the Social History books:

'On Sunday, and on Sundays only, we played with our Noah's Ark, which during the rest of the week stood high and unheeded on the inaccessible Ararat of the very top bookshelf. It contained, besides Noah and his family, some eighty couples of animals and birds, very sketchily carved and coloured. Still, you

are ferrets! Where can I have dropped them, I wonder?" Alice guessed in a moment that it was looking for the nosegay and the pair of white kid gloves, and she began hunting for them, but they were now nowhere to be seen — everything seemed to have changed since her swim in the pool, and her walk along the river-bank with its fringe of rushes and forget-me-nots, and the glass table and the little door had vanished.

Soon the rabbit noticed Alice, as she stood looking curiously about her; and at once said in a quick angry tone, "why, Mary Ann! what are you doing out here? Go home this moment, and look on my dressing-table for my gloves and nosegay, and fetch them here, as quick as you can run, do you hear?" and Alice was so much frightened that she ran off at once, without

head in the lap of the other, in such a manner that she can see nothing. Her companion claps her several times on the

back, holding up one or more fingers, saying,

"Mingledy, mingledy, clap, clap,
How many fingers do I hold up?"

She must endeavour to guess. If she guesses three, when in reality only two have been held up, her playmate says,

"Three you said, and two it was.
Mingledy, mingledy, clap, clap,
How many fingers do I hold up!" (holding up four.)

She guesses again, and whenever she guesses rightly, it becomes her turn to hold up her fingers, while her companion lays her head down and covers her eyes. She who holds up

From *Chatterbox* 1892 and
The Boys' Own Annual, 1888

Right, top: Flashman's Defeat—
illustration from *Tom Brown's
Schooldays; centre:* From GA
Henty's *In Times of Peril; below:*
The Playing Fields of Eton, from
Recollections of Eton, 1870

could distinguish one breed from another readily enough. The elephants had trunks; the tigers and zebras, orange and black stripes respectively; the camels, one hump; the dromedaries, two. The horses had long tails; the giraffes, long necks. So that if all the animals' heads were almost, and their legs exactly, alike, what of it?

'The most charming creatures were the birds. The raven, the thrush, the goldfinch and the rest were the same size, but we knew one from another—its blackness, its spotty breast, its red and yellow head, and so forth. The humans also had a striking family resemblance. They had identical black eyes and eyebrows, scarlet mouths, and no noses; round heads and no necks. But the males wore straight-down garb, whereas the females were pinched in at the waist; and Noah and Mrs Noah had wider-brimmed hats than their sons and daughters-in-law. They suited us on Sundays, just as the brick people did on weekdays, having the same blessed unobtrusiveness that made them so adaptable. We began our play with the traditional "animals went in two by two", and then branched off into variations on Treasure Island or Swiss Family Robinson, or stories made up by ourselves, any of these being tolerably sabbatical so long as we remembered to call the leading characters Mr and Mrs Noah, Shem, Ham, and Japhet.

'We secretly hoped and prayed for rain on Sundays, not only because that excused us from the boredom of church, but because we loved our Sunday occupations. Also, if Sunday was wet, we were allowed, in addition to Noah's Ark and various suitable books such as *Line upon Line* and *Peep of Day*, the use of our paint boxes and brushes. Squabbles about paints, a spill of water, or an accidental smear on another child's face or pinafore might be overlooked on week-days, but on Sundays were a signal for the instant removal of the paint-boxes. So we were always very solemn over our Sunday painting, as indeed it became us to be, since we had to paint texts instead of old *Punch* illustrations, or things drawn out of our heads. These texts, each with a flower at the corner, were printed in outline and first of all we laid the one we had each selected on a cushion and pricked round the edges of every letter and flower with a pin (the pin went in and out at each prick with a pleasant tick-flop noise). Then we painted (for example) *Thou* red, and *God* blue; *Seest* yellow, and *Me* green. After tea we each carried our completed text downstairs, and presented it to some grown-up in the drawing room or the servants' hall. I wonder what they did with them?'

Street playgrounds

Cosy nurseries were not for everyone. For an increasing minority, certainly; but still a minority. For most children, play took place in the street.

Norman Douglas, author of *South Wind*, wrote a book on London street games: published in 1916, it looks back to the closing years of the nineteenth century. Douglas adopts the convention of introducing an observant, but probably fictitious, 'Mr Perkins', who talks to him over the occasional drink in the Three Swans about how things used to be.

What were these cockney children's toys? Whatever was to hand: all the boys, for instance, wore caps in those days:

'Here are some of the cap-names: Chimney-Pots (or Upsetting the Chimney); Hat Under the Moon; Mouse in Trap; Sausage; Knock him Down Donkey; Pull for the Shore Sailor; Sugar and Milk; Hop O' my Thumb; Touch-Cap. Nuts-in-Cap is played with caps and crackers (Spanish nuts); in Hitting the Sun you must throw your cap at your opponent's at about about twelve yards distance; other cap-games are Quoits (with folded-up caps), and Fire Engines, and Shying over the Moon, and Shooting the Stars, and Piling the Donkey, and Cap It, and Where's This Little Hat to go, and Sally round the Jampot (with piled-up caps), and Ball in Cap, and Run a Mile for a Half-penny, and Hook and Cap, and Hot Soup, and Fox Come out of your Den, and Throw Over, and Miller's Sack, and Whack Cap, and Hatching Eggs, and Under the Garter.'

From *Street Arabs* by Dorothy
Stanley née Tennant, illustrator,
1890

Exceptional, the wealth of cap games? Not really. Try tin cans:

'There are many tin-can games, such as Tin-Can Bump and Tin-Can Jump
and Tin-Can Catch and Tin-Can Fishing and Tin-Can Fetch it and Tin-Can
Racing and Tin-Can Go It and Tin-Can Touch and Tin-Can Hide It and Tin-
Can Have It and Cock-Shy and Catch the Rider and Pitching up the Wall. The
best of all of them is Tin-Can Copper (or Kick-Can Policeman).'

The more primitive the props, the better:

'By far the best children's games are those played with mud. Of mud you
make Pies, and Bridges, and Sticking-Bricks (against a wall), and Mud-Carts
(played with a tin-can), and Wells, and Tunnels, and Flower-Pots, and
Castles—in fact, anything you please. There's nothing like mud, when all is said
and done, and it's a perfect shame there isn't more mud about, nowadays; or
sand, at least. You should see them go for it, when the streets are up. Because the
park is too far away for most of them. And then, the fact of the matter is, our boys
don't much like playing in the park, anyhow; and the few who care about it aren't
allowed to go, because their mothers say "You've got no clothes". They prefer
the streets; and that's the truth, though you wouldn't believe it. For one thing,
the keeper is always coming up in the park and interfering; next, they can't find
kerbs and paving-stones there; next, it makes them wild to see other boys with
bats and things, when they have none.'

Despite this last caveat, Douglas concludes on a note of conventional wisdom;
'If you want to see what children can do, you must stop giving them things.
Because of course they only invent games when they have none ready-made for
them, like richer folks have—when, in other words, they've nothing in their
hands. As Mr Perkins said: "You can't play a ball game, if you haven't got a
ball", meaning that if you want to play, and have nothing to play with, you must
play at something that doesn't need anything. Give them bats and balls, and they
soon forget their Chinese Orders, and there's an end of Showing No Ivory, and
nobody thinks of Pulling out Father's Rhubarb, and The Old Devil may go to—
well, where he came from. That's what keeps them alive and "imaginative" (as
Aunt Eliza would say)—having nothing to play with.'

A pious half-truth—but one wonders what happened to the lad who didn't
actually like cap-games, or tin-can games, or mud.

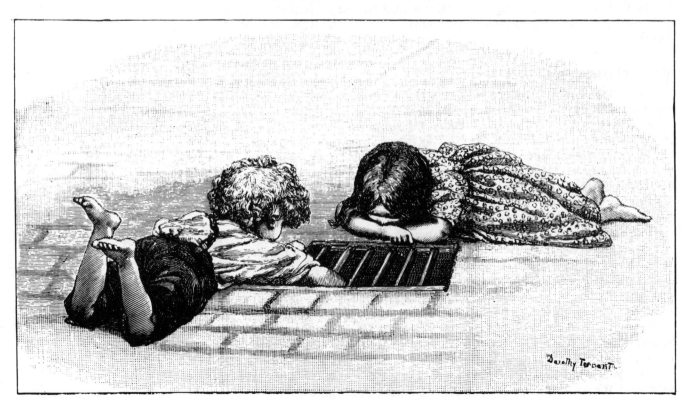

The daughters of Sir M. Decker, by Jan de Meyer, *Fitzwilliam Museum, Cambridge*

QUEEN ANNE'S TOYS

Queen Anne's toys

Facing top: The Blunt children, by Zoffany, *Birmingham City Art Gallery*

Below: The six eldest children of Frederick Prince of Wales, by du Pan

The eighteenth century was an age of contrasts. In the proportions of its domestic architecture, the elegance of its landscape gardening, the splendours of Gibbonian prose and the urbanity of conversation in Dr Johnson's circle, a new plateau of civilised living seems to have been reached; while Rousseau's idealisation of 'natural man' appears to usher in upon the Age of Enlightenment a new spirit of liberty also. Picture after picture in our galleries invests with a luminous serenity children and young people whose dress betokens a new-found freedom, a relaxed insouciance allied with an innocent gravity.

Such is the testimony of the century's legacy in art and literature: the stark realities of living were uglier. Beneath the enlightenment the rawest cruelties were practised and condoned. Men were hanged publicly for petty theft. Women were condemned to lifelong servility. Boys at sea were flogged for trivial offences. Little children were forced up chimney flues. Even those sensitive enough to deplore these things were rarely or never moved to take action to stop them. And the dying years of the century saw the children of the poor worse off, if anything, than earlier, as the mounting tide of industrialisation sucked more and more of them away from the monotonous but relatively humane daily round of the cottage craftsman into the harsh, impersonal regime of the factory overseer.

Nevertheless, new ideas were beginning to break surface which were destined eventually, after fitful advances and frequent retreats, to change out of all recognition the experience of childhood. Two short passages about the rearing of young children can serve to illustrate the persistence of old ideas and the emergence of new.

The first is from Dr William Buchan's *Domestic Medicine, or The Family*

Portrait of Cornelia Burch, 1581, artist unknown, *Scottish National Gallery*

156

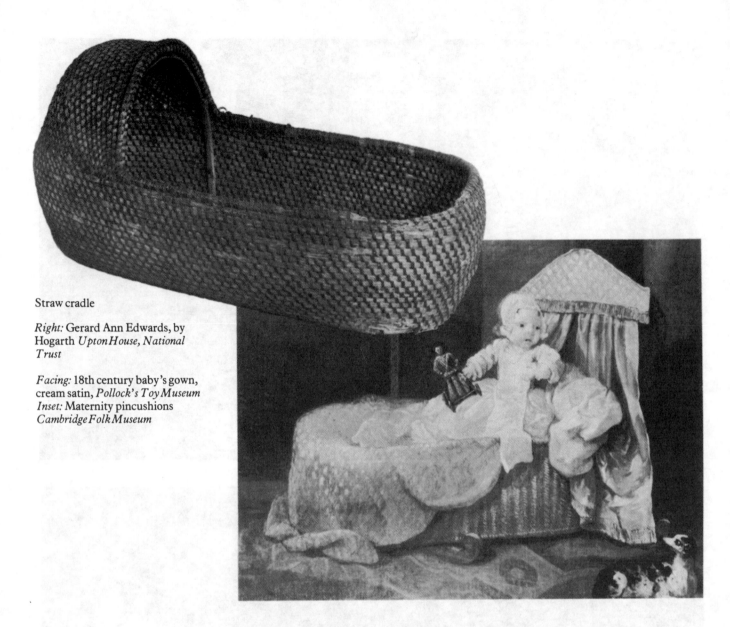

Straw cradle

Right: Gerard Ann Edwards, by Hogarth *Upton House, National Trust*

Facing: 18th century baby's gown, cream satin, *Pollock's Toy Museum* *Inset:* Maternity pincushions *Cambridge Folk Museum*

Physician, published in 1769. A pioneer in its field, the book became a bible to many mothers, an 18th century Dr Spock. It ran to nineteen editions (80,000 copies) in the author's lifetime, and was translated into most European languages.

'In many parts of Britain at this day a roller, eight or ten feet in length, is applied tightly round the child's body as soon as it is born. It is amazing how children escape suffocation, considering the manner in which they are often rolled up in flannels. I lately attended an infant whom I found muffled up over head and ears in many folds of flannel, though it was the month of June. Death, as might be expected, soon freed the infant of all its miseries.'

The second passage is from Jean-Jacques Rousseau's *Emile,* published in 1762:

'He is to live out of doors, to be allowed to run, even to fall. Emile shall have no head-pads, no go-cart, no leading-strings. The limbs of a growing child should be free to move easily in his clothes; nothing should cramp their growth or movement; there should be nothing tight, nothing fitting closely to the body, no belt of any kind. Defects of body and mind may all be traced to the same source: the desire to make men of them before their time.'

Practice had still to catch up with theory: Rousseau left five illegitimate children to be cared for by Paris Foundling Hospitals, where their nurture was hardly likely to be Rousseauesque. But his ideas took root.

158

Betsy and Susan (later Mrs Sibbald), daughters of Dr Thomas Mein, RN. From an enamel by Henry Bone after a painting by William Owen

Looking back

If childhood, at least by the end of the century, was beginning to be recognised, very little survives to suggest that people thought it worth recording, either of themselves or anyone else, what it was like to be a child. Painters have left a richer testimony than writers, but a testimony almost confined to the top stratum of society, and usually designed to appeal to the patron's vanity. Literature about childhood in any detail we hardly find until the next century, though sometimes it looks back from there to the later years of the eighteenth.

Susan Sibbald

The Memoirs of Susan Sibbald fall into this category. Born in 1783 at Fowey in Cornwall, she emigrated to Canada in her fifties and died there in 1866. At the age of seventy she wrote the memoirs which looked back over the first twenty-nine years of her life.

Susan was lucky both in the circumstances of her childhood and in the bubbling temperament which propelled her over whatever fences convention put in her way. She records with pride her prowess, out-matching the boys', at

160

spinning whip-tops; this apart, there is scarcely a reference, in hundreds of pages of childhood memories, to toys or playthings. What she remembers, and finds still memorable after the passage of over half a century, are the people whose lives impinged on hers, and her adventures: possessions, including dolls and toys, are of less significance, which is as it should be.

'The house in which we were all born was a commodious, but curious house. As it was built against the side of a rocky hill, to go to the nurseries, or above them to the children's parlour, or again above to the schoolroom, we had to climb a flight of granite steps, which was lighted by a glass roof on the inside of which were trained vines, the roots being in the garden above. Below the said rooms we were not allowed to appear, except of an evening, when we had to be dressed out for the occasion in coloured silk slips and thin muslin frocks—which were very suitable, as the moment we entered the drawing room, after our formal curtsies, we had to sit up all in a row, and as we were constantly told, "be silent, and look pretty, as children should be seen and not heard."'

'In those days children were sent from home to be nursed, and as my foster-mother was a smuggler's wife, no doubt I thought from my mother's dislike of me that I must have been changed, and that I was in reality a smuggler's child. At any rate, I could not but see myself that as my elder sisters had such beautiful fair complexions and lovely brown hair, and I so dark and with black hair, beside them I was not fit to be seen. Indeed Grace (the maid) used often to tell me I was "not fit to be seen", and when I came to be dressed before going downstairs

Lord Willoughby de Broke and his family, by Zoffany

The Ladies' Boarding School

frequently said my hair was "as straight as a pound of candles", and then taking down from the chimney-piece the great pinching-tongs and thrusting them into the fire, she would screw my hair in curl papers and pinch them with the hot tongs—an operation which I much dreaded.'

'One day after school, when we were all assembled on Place Walk as usual, our Governess and Capt. Dormer quietly seated below, and we promenading up and down arm-in-arm above, someone proposed we should go a little further off and run races. By and by the Donkeys (called Jackasses then) that had been carrying top dressing to the fields were put into one near us, their wooden panniers taken off their backs, and left to graze quietly, while the men went home to their dinners.

'"Now here is a chance," said one. "Let us have a ride!" "Joseph, you go," said another, "and bring one of the jackasses out. But where's a halter?" "Oh dear, well who has the strongest garters?" Mine were taken as being the newest, one of the animals brought, and by turns we rode up and down at some distance from the seat under the hedge . . . .

'But now I shudder to think of what we might have been guilty. For it was proposed—no doubt by the Dormers, who were jealous of their father's attention to our governess,—that we should go, so many on one side of the donkey, and so many on the other, and make him jump over their heads; no sooner said than done. Joseph Austin with his stick, and we with our frocks spread running at the poor beast simultaneously, he through terror took a leap over the bank. A roar from the Captain and a scream from his companion dispersed us all flying, non-stopping to look behind, the Dormers to their home, the Austins to Place, and we three scrambling through the hedges, and down the bank near the garden door, to our parlour.

'Now came our dinner-time, no governess to carve for us as usual. We feared some dreadful catastrophe had happened, and what would be the consequence? We however ate our dinners, and went up to our schoolroom consoling ourselves with the idea that if Miss Coade were not killed, she would not dare tell what had happened, as we were under her charge, and she ought not to have allowed us to

162

take the donkey, or be so riotous. Thus were we trying to calm our troubled spirits, when hark! Oh, how terrific to my ears was the not-uncommon sound of my god-mother's hammer-shaped heels on the garden steps, and approaching the schoolroom. The door was thrown open, and my heart died within me when first, without speaking a word, she held up my garters.

'"So!", she said, after feasting her eyes on my too apparently subdued person, and addressing me only, "You mother of all Mischief, you have lamed one of my jackasses. I have found out how it happened. Your garters were round his neck, so come off to the Tower!"'

At the age of twelve Susan Sibbald was packed off to boarding school at Bath—a school run by Miss Sophie Lee, author of *A Chapter of Accidents*, and her two sisters: they were friends of Mrs Siddons, Madame Piozzi and Sir Thomas Lawrence. Her debut found our tomboyish heroine true to form:

'Amongst lots of presents that had been given me at different times was a box of crayons of every colour and shade, which I liked better than anything else I had, and must needs take with me; but unfortunately, before putting them into my trunk with my clothes I had neglected to pack them properly, to prevent friction. Well, we arrived at The White Hart, Bath, and the next morning we were to go to Mrs Gambier's. When I went to my trunk to get a white frock, lo and behold, there were almost all my nice new clothes stained with red, black, yellow and green chalks.'

'We all had to speak French during school hours, or get "the mark" if we conversed in English. You were allowed, if you wished to know the name in French of any article, to mention the word in English, if you said before it "qu'est-ce le français pour". I often forgot to stop at the word, but ran on whole sentences in English, when the girl that had "the mark", or badge of misconduct, would say "Mais vous avez parlé anglais", and then hand it to me; and when I got it, which I am sorry to say was too often, I did not know how to pass it. I could not bear to give it to a girl I liked, and there were few indeed I did not like, but Mam'selle frequently assisted me. I was sure to feel unwell after the gruel (given as punishment). Many would take the sugar out of their cups and give it to me on leaving the dining room, which I dare say made me worse.'

Mam'selle, of course, was by definition 'old-fashioned', and had to be patronised by any self-respecting hoyden. Out walking one day, 'we had come to a stile in a field. When almost all were over, I had gone a little back to pick a flower in the hedge. She called me to come. By this time she and I were the only two on the road. "Dear me", she said, "here's a boy coming. I'll go over first, and you stand behind me and spread out your frock, and then the boy will not see me." He was approaching, and she was so long in getting over that I turned round to see what the boy was carrying, wondering whether it would be potatoes or apples he had in his bag? When she got down on the other side and saw that I had dropped my frock and was looking at the boy, who went on whistling and not caring to see or be seen, she told me how shockingly I had behaved, to be staring at boys in that way, and in allowing him to observe her going over the stile. Poor little woman, she was so short that she had hardly any leg to show, so that she need not have been so particular.'

'Lastly, the grand finale of the term: 'Just before the vacation came our ball— a great deal of excitement, of course, and preparation for this great event. I was told I was to dance a minuet that night, standing up with seven others of my own size, in one set, as in the present day for a double quadrille, but wider apart, each pair keeping separate from the others. It was quite laughable to see us on the terrace: instead of skipping round to keep ourselves warm, we were curtseying and sliding about, frocks held out, and going through all the movements as gracefully and as slowly as our shivering limbs would allow us, so anxious were we to "do credit to Bath".

'We were all to be dressed in book-muslin frocks, with primrose coloured sashes wide and long, and wreaths of roses of the same colour on our heads. The day before the ball came Mr Pope, the chief hairdresser in Bath, with two

163

assistants. We were called so many at a time into the room, where sat Miss Mangle, and as the fashion then was, our heads were to be dressed "à la Brutus". If it had been called "à la porcupine" or "à la hedgehog" it would have been as well, for except for the front row of curls around the face, which we were to put up ourselves as usual, the hairdressers screwed our hair up in innumerable curls all over our heads, and I am sure there never could have been seen at any time so many funny figures sit down to dinner . . . Fancy whether it would have been possible for us to rest our heads on our pillows, had they been even of down (which they certainly were not) with any comfort, when bristled all over with hard curl papers.

'The next day, immediately after dinner, came the uncurling process, and as the wreaths had to be put on after the dresses, so the girls left the hairdressers and came back to have the wreaths put on, and then they were ready to be sent

The Indian Emperor, by Hogarth, *Tate Gallery*

off to the Rooms. It took such a length of time before all could go, although each chair held two; but to tell you of my astonishment and disappointment when I came to have my wreath on would be impossible.

'When I saw Mr Pope take out of a box two rows of Roman pearls, I said, "Miss Mangle, these cannot be for me, certainly." "Oh yes miss," said Mr Pope, "Mrs Gambier brought them to me herself, and at the same time gave me a note for Miss Lee". "It is quite true my dear", said Miss Mangle, "Miss Lee told me. It was Mrs Gambier's request that you should wear them."

'I was in such a sad way about it. I was quite sure I would not be able to dance well. I should fear everyone would be looking at my conspicuous head; I was really ashamed to make my appearance before the girls, who were already dressed and waiting in the drawing room to be sent off as the chairs returned. A great many encouraged me and thought the beads so pretty; and I might have thought so too had not every other girl had on a wreath.'

Cecilia Siddons, by RJ Lane after Sir Thomas Lawrence

Cecilia Siddons

Sarah Siddons's daughter Cecilia went to the same school as Susan Sibbald, and was in the same class as Susan's younger sister, Fanny. If the bouncing, boisterous Susan seems often to have leapt out of a Restoration comedy clean through the 18th century conventions, Cecilia's notions of emancipation were the more predictable ones of an aspiring prima donna.

'One day', records Susan Sibbald, 'she seized her doll in her left hand and, holding it above her head, grasped something in her right as a dagger and rushed to the other side of the room. "This is the way Uncle John (Kemble) did in the character of Rollo when he crossed the bridge with Cora's baby, for one day I looked through the keyhole when he was rehearsing it before mama in our dining room." This very scene I witnessed afterwards at Drury Lane in the tragedy of Pizarro.

'She did not become an actress, however, but married Dr Coombe, the great phrenologist in Edinburgh, who wrote a great deal not only on that subject, but also on the management of children.'

Charles Lamb

'When we got in, and I beheld the green curtain that veiled a heaven to my imagination, which was soon to be disclosed—the breathless anticipations I endured! I had seen something like it in the plate pre-fixed to *Troilus and Cressida*, in Rowe's Shakespeare—the tent scene with Diomede; and a sight of that plate can always bring back in a measure the feeling of that evening. The boxes at that time, full of well-dressed women of quality, projected over the pit; and the pilasters reaching down were adorned with a glistering substance (I know not what) under glass (as it seemed), resembling—a homely fancy—but I judged it to be sugar-candy; yet to my imagination, divested of its homelier qualities it appeared a glorified candy! The orchestra lights at length arose, those 'fair Auroras'. Once the bell sounded. It was to ring out yet once again—and incapable of the anticipation, I reposed my shut eyes in a kind of resignation upon the maternal lap. It rang the second time. The curtain drew up—I was not past six years old—and the play was *Artaxerxes!*

'I had dabbled a little in the Universal History—the ancient part of it—and here was the court of Persia. I took no proper interest in the action going on, for I understood not its import—but I heard the word Darius, and I was in the midst of Daniel. All feeling was absorbed in vision. Gorgeous vests, gardens, palaces, princesses passed before me. It was all enchantment and a dream.'

Exotic and colourful, a feast for the eye and a bewilderment for the mind, *Artaxerxes* sounds like the very stuff on which the toy theatre was to feed so satisfyingly half a century later. But Charles Lamb's self-conscious stylistic artifice takes us away from, not into, the world of childhood; so that despite the enchantment, and the head in the maternal lap, he seems nearer at six years old to the mini-adult than to Rousseau's 'natural' child.

Dolls and dollmakers

18th century doll, *Lullingstone Castle, Kent*

Lord and Lady Clapham

On Friday 19th April 1974, at Sotheby & Co's Bond Street auction rooms, a Swiss lady bought twelve old dolls. For two of them she paid £16,000. They were described in the sale catalogue thus:

'*A pair of William and Mary male and female wooden dolls and their armchairs.* Both the Dolls' heads with delicately painted eyes and eyebrows, scarlet lips and well-rouged cheeks, the bodies with well-modelled hands and legs jointed at the hips and knees, both 22 inches high.

'He wears an auburn wig, lace-trimmed white cotton shirt, a pair of breeches in floral silver tissue with two pockets, a matching waistcoat, a fringed lawn scarf, a scarlet woollen jacket with silver-thread buttons and two pockets, his knitted white silk stockings with wine-coloured clocks and with buckled black leather shoes.

'His contemporary accessories comprise:

a black felt three-corner Hat, bearing the trade label of *T Bourdillon, Hosier and Hatter to His Majesty, No. 14 Russell Strt;, Covt. Gdn.;*

a pair of white kid Gloves:

a Sword with gilt-wire handle and leather Scabbard;

a silver-thread brocade drawstring Purse:

a Dressing Gown in coral satin brocaded with scrolling flowers in white and different colours and lined in pale blue Chinese silk damask.

'She wears a fair wig and spotted muslin fontage wired and trimmed with lace and pink ribbon, a white cotton shift, a white quilted cotton petticoat and her silver tissue stomacher made of the same material as her husband's waistcoat and breeches, her petticoat and Mantua in Chinese white satin damask with a design of flowers and leaves, her stockings matching her husband's and with silver-thread brocade shoes.

'Her contemporary accessories comprise:

a white cotton Night Shift;

a Petticoat and Dressing Gown matching her husband's dressing gown;

a very rare black silk mask with glass bead in the mouth.

'Their original armchairs in caned beechwood and elmwood, each with a leaf-carved toprail, turned supports, legs and stretchers, both 21 ins high.'

No one had ever paid such a sum for a doll. After a day or two of shocked silence the Victoria and Albert Museum decided to launch a public appeal to raise money to buy these dolls back from the purchaser, and to ask the Reviewing Committee on the Export of Works of Art to prevent their leaving the country for three months.

The money was found, the Swiss lady generously relinquished her hold, and Lord and Lady Clapham have since been on view in the Costume Gallery of the Victoria and Albert Museum.

The stolen dolls: a court case in 1733

No one knows where or by whom the Clapham dolls were made; nor the other ten rather less distinguished dolls which accompanied them to the sale room, and which included three 18th century wooden dolls. These would have been shaped, like the Clapham dolls, on the turner's lathe, the limbs being added separately to the skittle-shaped head and body (as with Queen Victoria's 'Dutch' dolls); and a case recorded in the Proceedings at the Sessions of the Peace for 1733, and recalled by Alice K Early in her book *English Dolls, Effigies and Puppets*, gives us a glimpse of a dollmaker at work at that time.

In April 1733 Joseph Phips and Jane Tinsley were indicted for stealing '14 naked babies (ie dolls) and 2 dozen of dressed babies, and one jointed baby', the goods of William Higgs. Here is part of William's testimony:

'I am a turner by trade, but my chief business is to make babies, and when they are made my wife dresses them. My boy and my journeywoman followed

166

Left: Lord and Lady Clapham

Below: A Queen Anne papier maché doll with wooden body. The habit is that of a choir nun of the Benedictine Order, and the nun unfrocked

the same sort of work; she lodged with one Margaret Davis, and was very intimate with one Joanna Morgan. My wife, going to Davis's house, found one of my matted chairs there; Davis said she bought it of my apprentice for ten pence tho' it stood me in fourteen pence . . .

'Upon this I got a search warrant, and found fourteen of my own babies in Tinsley's room in Davis's house. I know my own babies from any other man's; I can swear to my own work, for there's never a man in England that makes such babies besides myself. Then I went to Joanna Morgan's in the Minories, and there I found two dozen more of babies ready dressed in a basket, and these were my own work too.'

From this we learn that four people—Willam, his wife, his apprentice and his journeywoman—earned their living primarily by making dolls for the trade. William took pride in his work, and claimed to have his own techniques which distinguished his dolls from other people's. We are later told that he marketed his goods by selling them to shops or warehousemen. Two shops belonging to merchants are mentioned—one in St Catharine's Lane, the other Mr Robottom's in White-Chapel. He got fifteen shillings for half a gross, or 2½d apiece. Not a princely sum, but a good deal better than Mayhew's poverty-stricken toilers were earning some 120 years later. The whole little episode reflects an age when cottage industry could still offer the artisan a life of some dignity. As to the quality of William's products, we can only guess; but they were probably not very much different from the Clapham dolls, whose distinction lies in their age and their accoutrements rather than their craftsmanship.

167

The toy trade

Markets & Fairs

Playthings, such as they were, in the 18th century were still bought mainly in the open air—at markets and fairs. Fairs, of course, provided traditional entertainments too—including not yet Punch and Judy (Judy did not emerge till the 19th century), but an increasingly individualised and English Punch, larking with the devil rather than with a string of sausages, and no longer simply the imported Pulcinello whom Pepys had witnessed in the Restoration.

Toyshops

Besides the markets and fairs, we find numerous references to 'toyshops' in advertisements surviving from the 18th century. But a toy then meant any trifle or curiosity, and the proprietor of such a shop was fittingly described, in an article in *The British Toymaker* of November 1916, as 'an Autolycus of retail trade, a snapper-up of unconsidered trifles'.

'For a century', the article goes on, 'he, and she, for there were women in the business, must have made a pretty good thing out of it. Pepys, who was an incorrigible shopper, makes no direct reference to the toyshop, and the term seems to have originated somewhat later. By 1710, when *The Spectator* was being published, the toyshop had come into its own, as the advertisements in that journal testify. These shops were dotted about the City and extended westwards

Dissected map, *Pollock's Toy Museum*

Trade card for geographical game
and 18th century board games,
Pollock's Toy Museum

169

At the GREEN PARROT, *near* Chancery-Lane, Holborn;

IOHN·IACKSON·

ALEXANDER BURGES,

into the Strand. St Paul's Churchyard shadowed Mr Payn's toyshop at the Angel and Crown, where was sold "a famous Bavarian red liquor" which gives such a delightful blushing colour to the cheeks. A little lower down the street, at the Rose and Crown, under St Dunstan's Church in Fleet Street, Mrs Osborne sold at 2s 6d per bottle "an admirable chymical secret for the prevention of vapours in women". This connection between nostrums and cosmetics is insistent during the early years of the century. Another direction in which the toyman turned his activities was that of obtaining subscriptions for engravings.

'There is a very lively account of a toyshop of the period in a forgotten play, written by Robert Dodsby, bookseller, publisher, and playwright. It was produced at Covent Garden on February 3rd 1735, and is entitled *The Toyshop.* The interior of the shop is most skilfully suggested. The proprietor stands behind the counter, and to him comes a succession of customers. To one he advances money on watches and jewellery, and for each and all he has a word appropriate to their business. The customers represented include a woman wanting a mirror, another asking for a little box, a bevy of ladies in search of a stuffed dog, and a gentleman needing an ivory pocket book. A woman tries a mask, and a doddering old buck tries spectacles with tortoiseshell and silver rims. There is no actual reference to games or playing toys, but it is clear that the stock is remarkably varied.'

During the course of the century Birmingham became established as the centre of the steel 'toy' industry, including such products as corkscrews, buttonhooks, buckles, stilettos and bodkins; while in 1800 a handsome Directory to the city was published which contained 335 names in its Business section, twenty-four of these being the names of firms engaged in 'toy' production. Wood, ivory, glass, steel, silver and gold were among the materials used; while the output included pencil cases, buttons, snuffers, watch chains, snuffboxes, gilt trinkets, steel buckles, plating and jewellery.

In the early diary of Fanny Burney we learn that the author received in 1773 a commission from her stepsister to buy for her husband 'two cricket balls made by Pett of 7 Oaks. You will get them at any of the great toyshops, the maker's name always stamp'd upon them—ask for the very best sort, which costs 4s or 4s 6d each. Let them be 4 oz and ¼ or 4 oz and ½ each; send them by the Exeter post coach.' By then, therefore, several London shops apparently carried sports equipment as part of their regular stock.

In some shops, by now, 'toys' in the sense of children's playthings were beginning to be found too. In High Holborn, for instance, there was Hamley's precursor, the Noah's Ark, and the Green Parrot, which advertised 'fine babies (ie dolls) and baby-houses'—though only as a postscript to a long list stretching from microscopes to crystal sleeve buttons and fortune telling cards. *Gulliver's Travels,* as early as 1726, has a reference to 'a London toyshop for the furniture of a babyhouse'; while other surviving trade cards advertise 'all sorts of English and Dutch toys with all sorts of naked and dressed babies', and 'Bristol toys in general such as coaches, wagons etc' at 1d and 2d.

At MARTIN'S Toy and Cap-Shop,

The THREE RABBITS *near* Durham-Yard
in the Strand;

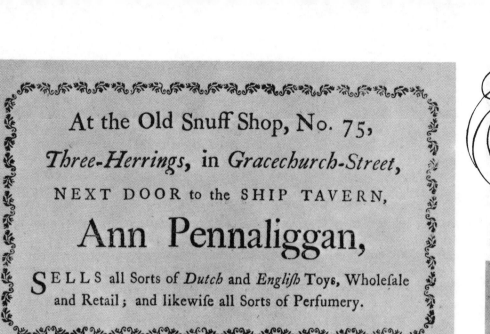

At the Old Snuff Shop, No. 75,

Three-Herrings, in *Gracechurch-Street*,

NEXT DOOR to the SHIP TAVERN,

Ann Pennaliggan,

SELLS all Sorts of *Dutch* and *English* Toys, Wholesale
and Retail; and likewise all Sorts of Perfumery.

Details from trade cards

171

Tangram, Tunbridge ware,
Pollock's Toy Museum

Top right: 19th century Tunbridge
ware, mosaic wood, *Tunbridge
Wells Museum*

Centre: Two early Tunbridge ware
housewives

Below: Nesting boxes, Tunbridge
ware. The labels had the names of
different spas printed on them: 'A
Present from . . .'

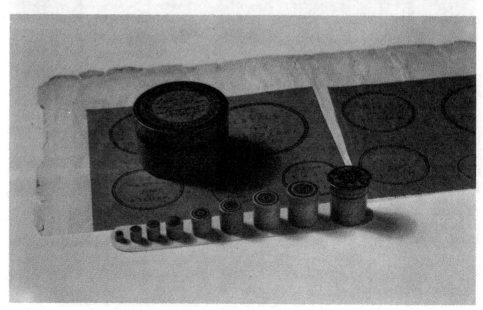

Two pottery money boxes, late 18th century, *Pollock's Toy Museum*

A country toy industry: Tunbridge Ware

It would be a mistake to imagine the toy industry, in the eighteenth century, as centred solely or even mainly on the larger cities such as London and Birmingham. England was still a land of villages and small market towns; and the raw materials of some playthings were ready to hand in the country.

In the Weald of Kent, for instance, around Tunbridge Wells, there had always been a plentiful supply of timber from the abundant woods and orchards: it had been used since early times for making barrels, pails and other household utensils. By the eighteenth century, however, Tunbridge Wells had also become a fashionable spa. Charles II and his Queen visited it in 1663, and during the Great Plague of London two years later many of the nobility made it their headquarters. Macaulay says that 'during the season a kind of fair was held daily near the fountain' and that 'milliners, toymen and jewellers came down from London and opened a bazaar under the trees'. This no doubt acted as a spur to the local shopkeepers to develop locally made, specialty woodware, suitable for souvenirs; for Celia Fiennes, visiting the spa in 1697, describes 'the shopps full of all sorts of toys, silver, china, millinery, and all sorts of curious wooden ware, which this place is noted for'.

Seventy years later, in 1766, Benge Burr in his *History of Tunbridge Wells* describes this 'curious wooden ware' as he knew it in more detail:

'The trade of Tunbridge Wells is similar to that of Spa in Germany, and chiefly consists in a variety of toys in wood, such as tea-chests, dressing-boxes, snuff-boxes, punch-ladles and numerous other little articles of the same kind. Of these great quantities are sold to the company in the summer, and especially at their leaving the place, when it is customary for them to take Tunbridge fairings to their friends at home.

'The wood principally used for this purpose is holly, which grows in great abundance in the surrounding country, and furnishes a prodigious variety of the prettiest ornamental inlays that can be imagined, some of which are so excellent in their kind, that it is hard to believe they are not assisted by the pencil. But besides holly they use no small quantity of cherry-tree, plum-tree, yew and sycamore; the yew specially is of late become very fashionable, and the goods veneered with it are certainly excessively pretty.'

Tunbridge Wells was producing in the eighteenth century, besides these elegant trifles which became more and more intricately patterned with mosaics of different wood veneers, a number of wooden 'toys' as we understand the word: bilboquets, tops, yoyos, cribbage and Pope Joan boards, for instance. These were delicately made, but simply ornamented with painted sprigs of

173

leaves, flowers, or coloured bands. And on the list of wares purveyed at the turn of the century by Mr J Robinson, self-styled 'Tunbridge Ware Manufacturer, Print-seller, and Perfumer to their Royal Highnesses' we find, tucked in among the scents, cosmetics, corn plasters, blacking-cakes, and True Blue liquid for cleaning the tops of boots and saddles,—'Best Cricket-Bats and Balls'.

Cricket had in fact by 1800 attained a status more dignified than its association with perfumes and pomades in a retailer's list would suggest. We have earlier recorded Fanny Burney's commission to buy two cricket balls at neighbouring Sevenoaks; and cricket had been played here and there under recognised rules throughout the century: indeed, as early as 1744 the county of Kent, in which Tunbridge Wells stands, had played a famous match at Finsbury, London, against All England. The year 1787 had seen the creation of the prestigious Marylebone Cricket Club, the game's high priest throughout its subsequent history; while its cherished epic and moral qualities had already been celebrated in a poem dedicated to the Richmond Cricket Club:

> 'Hail Cricket, glorious, manly, British game,
> First of all Sports, be first alike in Fame!'

The British—or rather, the English—did indeed develop the game, propagate it, near-deify it. Did they originate it? Consult an English source, and you will be referred to the accounts of King Edward I, alluding to a game of 'creag', or to mediaeval texts featuring a 'cricce' (a curved bat); consult a French, and you will learn that it derives of course from 'criquet', a French word, and that French references antedate English by 100 years. Never mind, England—you owned half of France anyway in those days, didn't you?

Bookshops

Books are naturally better survivors than toys or dolls; but as Muir in his classic work on English Children's Books tells us, before the 18th century there were 'few books written expressly for the entertainment of children, who were thus compelled to select from the reading of their elders anything that especially appealed to them'. Where did children find these books?

Caxton translated *Aesop's Fables* from the French and printed them in 1484; and next year he produced the first printed edition of Malory's story of *King Arthur and the Knights of the Round Table*. Other romances and legendary tales like *Jack the Giant Killer* and *Dick Whittington* were sold by pedlars at country fairs and in towns and villages, together with other articles useful or attractive to housewives. These pedlars, or chapmen as they were called, would carry in their packs a selection of cheap little books and ballad sheets, often folded into miniature booklets of eight or twelve pages comprising also collections of

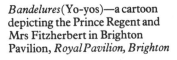

Bandelures (Yo-yos)—a cartoon depicting the Prince Regent and Mrs Fitzherbert in Brighton Pavilion, *Royal Pavilion, Brighton*

174

Miniature Tunbridge Wells bats
and stumps, with a notice of a
cricket match, 1795

The Children of Hugh and Sarah
Wood, by Joseph Wright of Derby,
Derby Museum

riddles, cooking recipes and often ribald comic stories. These 'chapbooks' were not produced with children in mind, but they were the only literature widely available to them—or for that matter to adults.

Even these chapbooks were banished during the years of Puritan domination in England. Dedicated as the Puritans were to the conviction that religion should form the basis of all human activities, they set about indoctrinating the young with a rigour as harsh as it was humourless. The books which they produced for the pious edification of them and their elders were all boring in the extreme, with one exception: *The Pilgrim's Progress*, by John Bunyan, first published in 1678 and read ever since as an adventure story where the hero battles with giants and monsters.

The English translations of Perrault's fairy stories, Daniel Defoe's *Robinson Crusoe*, and Swift's *Gulliver's Travels* were all written for a much wider public than children; and it was not until the mid-18th century that a number of enterprising publishers started to produce small illustrated books for the juvenile market. One of the most successful was J Newbery, who in June 1744 placed an advertisement in the *Penny Morning Post* for:

'A Little Pretty Pocket Book, intended for
the instruction and amusement of Little Master
Tommy and Pretty Miss Polly, with an agreeable
letter to read from Jack the Giant Killer.
Printed by J. Newbery, at the Bible and
Crown, near Devereux Court, without Temple Bar.
Price of the book alone 6d
with a ball or pincushion 8d.'

Newbery was a self-educated and ambitious man. He soon moved his business to St Paul's Churchyard, the traditional centre of the book trade. Here he became the friend of both Johnson and Goldsmith; and his descendants carried on the work he had begun of producing books designed specifically to attract young readers.

Geographical games

If children could be cajoled into reading and enjoying books, were there not other ways also of exploiting this new market by combining entertainment with instruction? John Jeffreys, a writing master and geographer living in Westminster in the 1750s, hit on the idea of adapting to this purpose the traditional game of Goose—ancestor of all our well-known 'travelling' games such as Ludo or Snakes and Ladders. He took a map of Europe and made it into a race game in which rival 'travellers were moved along a track through all the countries by the throw of a dice.'

An elaborate Explanation, in engraved lettering over the Atlantic Ocean, instructs the players what to do on arrival at each of the 77 numbered places. Thus No 28, Hanover, is the foot of a 'ladder': 'He who rests at 28 at Hanover shall by order of Ye King of Great Britain who is Elector, be conducted to No 54 at Gibraltar to visit his countrymen who keep garrison there'. But No 48, Rome,

Ellen, a paper cut-out dressing doll, from AT Tuer's *Forgotten Children's Books*

Facing: From AT Tuer's *Forgotten Children's Books*

176

When they had taken off a great deal of Cotton and
Paper, they found.—what do you think? a very large wax doll

I must not ugly faces scrawl

With charcoal on a white-wash'd wall.

Troublesome Cecilia.

5   Skipping.

6   Hunt the Slipper.

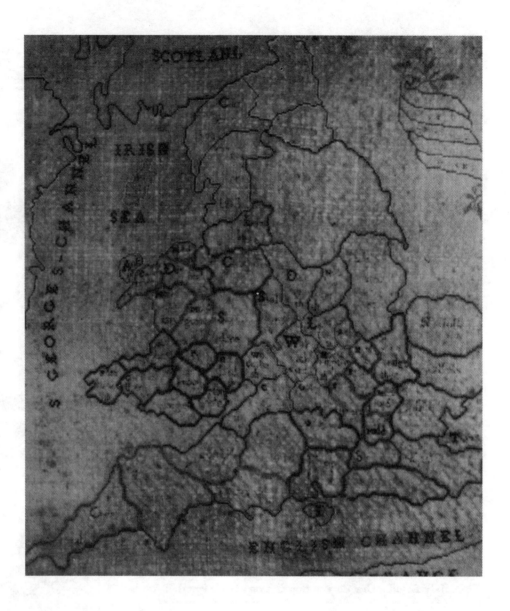

Sampler of Map of England,
Pollock's Toy Museum

is of course the head of a 'snake': 'He who rests at 48 at Rome, for kissing ye Pope's toe shall be banished for his folly to No 4 on the cold island of Iceland and miss three turns'. Subtle instruction, therefore, not only in geography but in contemporary history and in the true religion as well.

This, the earliest dated game known, was advertised as 'A Journey through Europe, or The Play of Geography. Invented and sold by the proprietor, John Jeffreys, at his house in Chapel Street, near the Broad Way, Westmr. Writing Master, Accompt., Geographer, etc. Printed for Carrington Bowles, Map and Printseller, No 69 in St Paul's Churchyard, London. Price 8s. Published as the Act directs, September 14th, 1759'. The engraved map, measuring 27 × 20 inches, was cut into sixteen sections, mounted on canvas, and folded into a cardboard slip case in the manner of travelling maps of the period.

Just up the road from Westminster, at Charing Cross, another Jeffreys, Thomas, had his business. Presumably a relative of John's, though we do not know for certain, he was not only a cartographer, but Geographer to the King. In 1770 he published a similar game; and using the promotional handle his privileged position gave him he called it 'The Royal Geographical Pastime exhibiting a Complete Tour through England and Wales', and dedicated it to the Prince of Wales.

Before Thomas Jeffreys could bring his Tour of England to birth, however, a young apprentice of his, John Spilsbury, had had, and acted on, an even brighter

178

idea. He mounted a map of England on thin mahogany board, cut it along the county boundaries, and sold it, boxed, for children to re-assemble. By 1763 he had set up in business in Russell Court, off Drury Lane, sharing premises with his elder brother Jonathan who was already a successful portrait painter and mezzotint engraver.

A London street directory for 1763 contains the following entry in its 'Alphabetical List of the Masters and Professors of the Polite and Liberal Arts and Sciences':

'Spilsbury, John. Engraver and Map Dissector in wood, in order to facilitate the Teaching of Geography. Russel-Court, Drury Lane.

A trade card he issued about this time lists no less than twenty-eight different dissected maps available from him, including The World, the known continents, most European countries, and the West Indies. These dissected maps—the prototypes of the jigsaw puzzle—seem therefore to have found a ready market; but John Spilsbury died young, his immediate successors showed little interest in his invention, and twenty years passed before it was developed a stage further. William Cowper's *John Gilpin* had proved a gold-mine to the printsellers, and illustrations to it soon flooded the market. Why should dissections be confined to school matter, someone asked? Why not dissect John Gilpin, and have fun re-assembling him?

With *John Gilpin*, then *Tristram Shandy*, the dissected puzzle was steered away from teaching and towards popular toy. But Jeffreys and Spilsbury had built a bridge between education and play which, tenuous enough and often unrecognised through the next century, was to bring startling developments in both in the twentieth. The imaginative leaps which led the bookish Jeffreys to adapt a gambling game to educational ends, and Spilsbury the friend of artists and engravers to ally high quality design with a new technique which encouraged learning by doing, were within their smaller range as significant as the new ideas which have sprung from the interplay of the teacher's and the toymaker's crafts in more recent years. We can imagine the precocious Charles Lamb, to pass the dawdling hour before it was time to leave for *Artaxerxes*, toying with a Spilsbury dissection which was already child's play to him; just as children ever since have whiled away hour after hour at jigsaws, first to puzzle them out, then again and again to display their cleverness now to themselves, now to admiring peers or adults.

Miniature tea set, *Pollock's Toy Museum.* Similar 'toy' tea and dinner services were produced from mid-18th century onwards by many porcelain factories: Bow, Worcester, Lowestoft, Caughley, Leeds, Wedgwood and Spode among them

179

Detail from A Family Group, by Coques, *National Gallery*

KING CHARLES, QUEEN BESS
AND BEYOND

Lady Arbella Stuart, aged 23
months, *Hardwick Hall, Derbyshire*

King Charles, Queen Bess, and beyond

It was tough being a child in Stuart or Tudor times: the higher you were up the social scale, the tougher, probably; and toughest of all if you were near the throne. Arbella Stuart was less than two when, in 1577, she was dolled up for this picture. She was to spend a stormy adolescence incarcerated by her grandmama in Hardwick Hall. She died prematurely, out of her mind.

Lady Jane Grey actually sat on the throne—for nine days, and was then executed. She bore her harsh childhood more stoically than Arbella, for she was fortunate in her schoolmaster, if in nothing else. Roger Ascham, Princess Elizabeth's tutor, once found Jane in a window-seat reading Plato, and was amazed that so young a girl knew so much Greek and took such pleasure in learning. He asked Jane how she had come by her knowledge.

182

'I will tell you', said Jane. 'One of the greatest benefits that God ever gave me is that He sent me with sharp, severe parents so gentle a schoolmaster. When I am in the presence of either father or mother, whether I speak, keep silent, sit, stand or go, eat, drink, be merry or sad, be sewing, playing, dancing or doing anything else, I must do it so perfectly as God made the earth; or else I am so sharply taunted, so without measure misordered that I think myself in Hell—till the time comes when I must go with Mr. Aylmer, who teacheth me so gently, so pleasantly and with such pure allurements to learn, that I can think all the time of nothing else while I am with him.'

Elizabeth herself was so neglected as a child after her mother Anne Boleyn's execution that her governess had to send an appeal for clothes for her to the King. 'She hath neither gown or kirtle' wrote Lady Byron, 'nor petticoat, nor no manner of linen, nor fore-smocks, nor kerchiefs, nor rails, nor body stitchets, nor handkerchiefs, nor sleeves, nor ruffles, nor biggens'. Still, she survived, perhaps not altogether displeased to be without some of them. Of Catherine of Aragon's ten children, just one lived to adulthood.

Looking back

To see her reading Plato at seven does not put us off Lady Jane; rather it endears her to us, combined as it is with such warmth of feeling and delicacy of utterance. Abhorrent, by contrast, to the twentieth century reader is the paternal pride with which John Evelyn dilates upon the precocious accomplishments, at an even earlier age, of a son destined to die in childhood.

John Evelyn on his son

'At two years and a half old he could perfectly read any of the English, French, Latin or Gothic letters, pronouncing the first three languages exactly. He had before his fifth year, or in that year, not only skill to read most written hands, but to decline all the nouns, conjugate the verbs regular and most of the irregular; got by heart almost the entire vocabularie of Latine and French primitives and words, could make congrous syntax, turn English into Latin and vice versa, construe and prove what he read, and did the government and use of relatives, verbs, substantives, eclipses and many figures and tropes; began himself to write legibly, and had a strong passion for Greek,. He was apt in ingenious application of tables and morals, for he had read Aesop; had a wonderful disposition to mathematics, having by heart divers propositions of Euclid that were read to him in play; while as to his piety, astonishing were his applications of scripture upon occasion, and his sense of God; he had learn'd all his Catechisms early, and understood the historical part of the Bible and New Testament to a wonder. Alas, he died suffocated by the women and maids that tended him, and covered him too hot with blankets as he lay in a cradle, near an excessive hot fire in a close room.'

Dying was so much a child's business in those days that children were quite aware of their probable fate; and this child called his father to him and told him that 'for all I loved him so dearly, I should give my house, land, and all my fine things to his brother Jack.'

Lucy Hutchinson

Lucy Hutchinson was born Lucy Apsley, eldest daughter of Sir Allen Apsley, Lieutenant of the Tower of London, in 1619. A fragment of autobiography, written fifty years later, survives: it tells of a childhood remarkable chiefly for priggishness, relieved in her case by the element of informal education provided by her mother's maids:

'When I was about seven years of age, I remember I had at one time eight tutors in several qualities—languages, music, dancing, writing and needlework; but my genius was quite averse from all but my book, and that I was so eager of that my mother, thinking it would prejudice my health, would moderate me in

Roanoke Indian child, 1585, holding doll brought by English colonists to America. Painting by John White, *British Museum*

183

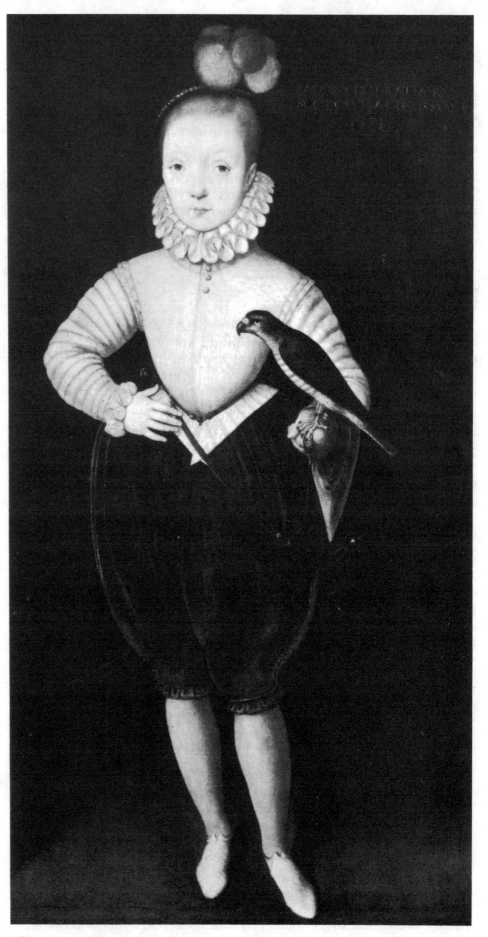

James I. Painting attributed to R Lockey after A van Brounkhorst, 1574, *National Portrait Gallery*

184

it. Yet this rather animated me than kept me back: after dinner and supper I still had an hour allowed me to play, and then I would steal into some hole or other to read. My father would have me learn Latin, and I was so apt that I outstripped my brothers who were at school, although my father's chaplain, that was my tutor, was a pitiful dull fellow.

'As for music and dancing, I profited very little in them, and would never practise my lute and harpsichords but when my masters were with me; and for my needle, I absolutely hated it. Play among other children I despised, and when I was forced to entertain such as came to visit me, I tired them with more grave instructions than their mothers, and plucked all their babies to pieces, and kept the children in such awe that they were glad when I entertained myself with elder company, to whom I was very acceptable.

'Through the good instruction of my mother, and the sermons she carried me to, I was convinced that the knowledge of God was the most excellent study, and accordingly applied myself to it, and to practise as I was taught. I used to exhort my mother's maids much, and to turn their idle discourses to good subjects; but I thought, when I had done this on the Lord's Day, and every day performed my due tasks of reading and praying, that then I was free to anything that was not sin, for I was not at that time convinced of the vanity of conversation that was not scandalously wicked. I thought it no sin to learn or hear witty songs and amorous sonnets or poems, and twenty things of that kind, wherein I was so apt that I

Three children of James I, 1611
British School, artist unknown

became the confidant in all the loves that were managed among my mother's young women; and there was none of them but had many lovers.'

It is a relief to be able to turn from these prodigies to a tapestry of the 16th century which reassures us that some could, even then, not only recognise childhood but celebrate it. It depicts a child whipping a top, and beneath are these verses:

'I am called chyldhood, in play is all my mynde
To cast a coyte, a cokstele or a ball;
A top I can set and dryve it in its kynde;
But would to God these hatefull bokes all
Were in a fyre brent to pouder small.
Then myght I lede my lyfe alwayes in play,
Which God send me to myne endying day.'

Jaques's whining schoolboy would have sympathised.

Dolls

Bartholomew babies

The doll that Arbella Stuart was carrying in her posed portrait was richly dressed in Tudor clothes; it had a wig and a carved and painted face. Her stiff skirt perhaps conceals the fact that she had no legs, but only stiffened underskirts. The same type of doll reappears in the portraits of James I's children and of the Puritan girl—and indeed in the painting of the near naked Indian girl, who had no doubt been presented with her doll by an early Virginian settler.

Under their fine clothes and the paint on their faces, these dolls were perhaps akin to the little wooden doll body found buried in the foundations of the old Christ's Hospital school for boys and girls in Newgate Street, London, when it was pulled down in 1902. This shaped torso has delicately carved features, and traces of gesso under the thick coat of 20th century varnish which now covers it. The head is covered with a loosely woven, or perhaps even finely knitted, material. Rows of stitching indicate where the hair for the wig was sewn on; while at the back two groups of threads show where the arms were attached, no doubt made of shaped soft leather or cloth, and stuffed with rag or sawdust.

The doll was possibly made before 1668—the year when the Newgate Street school was partially rebuilt after the Great Fire of London. We can imagine some pupil of the school dressing it in the blue gown and apron, with white coif and peak, which was the traditional dress of the Blue Coat girls since the foundation of their school in 1552—just as subsequent generations of pupils there have reproduced in miniature later editions of the school uniform of their day.

All these dolls have a strong family resemblance to those sold by pedlars at the great London fair held every autumn at Smithfield, outside the churchyard of St. Bartholomew's Priory. Our earliest pictorial record of toys on sale at this fair is a small engraving made in 1727 and reproduced in Henry Morley's *Memoirs of Bartholomew Fair*, published in 1874. Earlier and more ample written evidence of the range of things on sale at the toy booth comes, however, from Ben Jonson's comedy *Bartholomew Fair*, first performed in 1614—the year that the mushy ground of Smithfield was first paved over. Between his shows the puppet master, Lanthorn Leatherhead, cries his wares:

'What do you lack, what do you buy, pretty mistress? A fine hobby horse, to make your son a tilter? A drum to make him a soldier? A fiddle to make him a reveller? What is't you lack? Little dogs for your daughters? Or babies male or female?

'What do you lack, gentlemen? Fine purses, pouches, pin-cases, pipes? What is't you lack? A pair of smiths to wake you in the morning, or a fine whistling bird?'

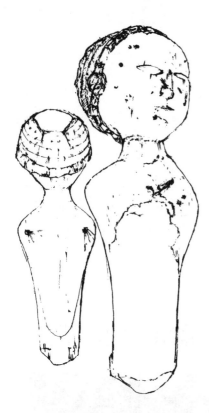

Doll excavated at Christ's Hospital, 1902, drawn by Debbie Brown

186

The rich, simple-minded country squire Cokes, who is throwing his money around buying presents for his tenant's children, has loaded his man-servant with rattles, pipes, and knives. He stops at Lanthorn Leatherhead's stall.

'Those six horses, friend, I'll have,' he says 'and the three Jew's trumps, and half a' dozen o' birds, and that drum (I have one drum already), and your smiths—I like that device of your smiths, very pretty well; and four halberts, and—let me see—that fine painted great lady, and her three women for state, I'll have.'

The sale is interrupted by Joan Trash, the gingerbread woman, but ends with Cokes buying her entire basket and all the toy stock for thirty shillings.

We have the list; we know the cost; but what exactly the items were we can only guess. Were the birds real live birds? Or lumps of roughly moulded, sun-baked clay stuck over with feathers, similar to those to be found until quite recently in peasant markets all over the Balkans? Or were they little pottery whistles which warble like birds when filled with water? Are Jew's trumps the same as Jew's harps? And what were smiths? Were they two crudely carved figures hitting a wooden anvil, similar to those still made by peasant craftsmen in Russia? And the dogs—were they like the sheep sold in later 18th century markets, simply shaped and covered with a bit of real dog's hair or lamb's wool? Or were they clay dogs? As for the great painted lady, she must surely have had affinities with Arbella Stuart's doll?

Another unanswered question is, where did the toys come from? Did Lanthorn Leatherhead make some of them himself, just as in all probability he made his own puppets? Or were they imported? Customs records show that consignments of dolls were certainly arriving in England by the early 16th century; and one entry in the indexes specifies 'Babies for children from Germany, brought with other toys such as wooden pipes, rattles and swords'—among the very items mopped up by Squire Cokes.

'Babies' did not become 'dolls' till the reign of William and Mary (the twentieth century, with characteristic verbal gluttony, has commandeered both words in turn for the adult female human). Henry Morley speculates interestingly on the origin of the word 'doll':

'The only lexicographer I know who indicates the modern origin of the word

Illustrations from John Morley's *Memoirs of Bartholomew Fair*, 1874

"doll" is Richardson. But even Richardson guesses the derivation of the word to be from the Dutch "dol"—senselessly. Nevertheless he quotes, as an old word of endearment, "pretty little doll-pol"—which is, but in brief, Dorothy Mary. Because to the fair sex belong pretty faces and gay dresses—and doubtless also for other reasons known to the toy-maker—dolls, with a few ridiculous exceptions, have at all times been feminine. So when some popular toyman, who might have called his babies pretty Sues, or Molls, or Polls, cried diligently to the ladies who bought fairings for their children "Buy a pretty Doll", the conquest of a clumsiness inherent in the name of "baby" was recognised. We have good reason to be tolerably certain that Bartholomew Fair gave its familiar name to a plaything now cherished in every English nursery.'

From AT Tuer's *History of the Horn Book*

Gingerbread

Joan Trash's edible gingerbread dolls, by contrast, present few problems to the 20th century researcher. According to a 14th century recipe they were made from rye flour, spices and honey. Why then does Zeal-of-the-Land Busy the Banbury Puritan explode with such deafening vehemence over the inoffensive Lanthorn Leatherhead and the gingerbread woman?

'I was moved in spirit to be here this day', he screams as he overturns Joan's basket, 'in this Fair, this wicked and foul Fair, to protest against the abuses of it . . . the merchandise of Babylon again, and the peeping of popery upon the stall there! See you not Goldilocks, the purple strumpet, there, in her yellow gown and green sleeves? The profane pipes, the tinkling timbrels? A shop of relics! And this idolatrous grove of images, this flasket of idols which I will pull down, in my zeal and glory to be thus exercised!'

Harmless cakes, but linked inextricably in the excited Puritan mind with the traditions of the Catholic Church's religious feast days. Honey, the only sweetener easily available in Europe until the late 16th centry, came from hives that also provided the wax for making candles to burn before the shrine of a saint. Indeed, even in Communist Hungary to-day the two trades of candlestick maker and decorative gingerbread maker are carried on side by side in many towns in the same family concerns.

Carved wooden gingerbread mould

189

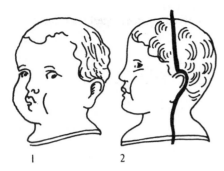

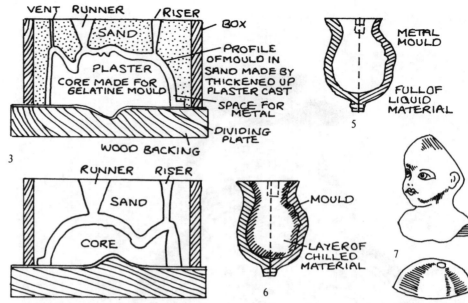

1   2

From an article on *How Wax Dolls are Made*, in *Work, the Illustrated Weekly Journal of Handicrafts*, 20 November 1915

1 & 2 Cast of moulded 'character' dolls' heads showing parting line
3 Type-metal mould for doll's head: obverse mould
4 Reverse mould
5 & 6 Chilled system of casting, before and after casting
7 Head with scalp removed
8 Cardboard scalp
9 Hair ready for insertion
10 Putting in hair
11 Hair in place

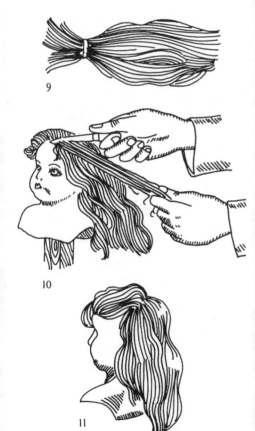

9

10

11

Right: Letitia Powell doll, 1761. Wax head, stuffed cloth body, ivory silk dress, *Victoria & Albert Museum*

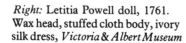

190

Wax works

Beautiful candles for the Church, and massive seals for charters and legal documents, were only two of the many uses of wax; for the ease with which it can be shaped and moulded when warm makes it also one of the simplest materials for fashioning human images. In Southern Germany and Austria shops that specialise in fashionable coloured candles and wax casts from old gingerbread moulds still sell at Christmas tiny infant Jesuses of wax; while in Spain and Portugal shops dealing in those huge white church candles, set amongst realistic bouquets of wax flowers, also offer fragile, hollow wax cats, dogs, babies and strange anatomical parts to take to church for reinforcing the message of one's prayer for the invalid human or animal. In Brussels, too, until a year ago a shop specialising in plaster saints, crucifixes and rosaries had drawers full of wax arms and coyly smiling heads for home-made shrines to the Virgin Mary.

These modern wax figures are survivals of a long tradition within the Catholic church. In the Musée Historique Lorrain in Nancy there is a gallery devoted to religious folk art parading serried ranks of doll-sized wax figures, brightly coloured and dressed, accompanied by an early eighteenth century trade card informing us that 'François Guillot makes saints male and female, richly dressed and framed; infant Jesuses of all sizes and in different attitudes, entirely of wax; or heads, feet and heads dressed, or ready to be dressed, with all the necessary names, and accessories such as animals, houses, birds, spangles, and shells of all kinds. He also supplies portraits of Princes and Princesses, heads for the Virgin Mary, and for country people curiosities of all kinds on request, of any size and moving or not, according to requirements. He also does portraits from life.'

In England, it is possible that Joan Trash's ancestors, like their continental counterparts, moulded wax images for sale at the great church festivals, along with medallions, amulets, plaster statues and other holy safeguards. What is certain is that Zeal-of-the-Land Busy and all his Puritan allies smashed the idols, defaced the great stone carvings and ornaments of the Church and drove the workers in wax to secret underground activities. The waxen image was no longer associated with prayer for a better life, but with the intent to do evil. Women accused of witchcraft because of their eccentric behaviour were alleged to have made waxen figures in the likeness of their victims and, by burning or defacing the wax, to have wrought ill upon them.

Modelling in wax survived in England, however, in another curious way also. From the 13th century onwards it was customary at the funerals of Kings or Queens or other great persons to represent them by a life-sized robed figure, either of wood or wax, which lay on the coffin as it was borne through the streets. The faces of these effigies were often carefully modelled death masks; and eighteen of them have survived and are on view in the Norman Undercroft of Westminster Abbey. They include a frighteningly realistic wax effigy of Queen Elizabeth I, and a charming one of 'La Belle Stuart'—Frances, Duchess of Richmond and Lennox and the original of the figure of Britannia on British coins. Her waxen image was made at her own request by Mrs Goldsmith in 1702, immediately after her death, at a cost of £260.

In another case, by his mother's side, stands Robert, Marquess of Normanby, who died at the age of three in 1715. He wears a red velvet coat, slit at the back for leading strings, and a long, yellow silk waistcoat over a tiny corset; and he sports a lace cravat and an elaborate cap. We do not know who modelled this charming child: it may well have been the famous Mrs Goldsmith, who was almost certainly responsible for the effigies of William III and his Queen Mary.

Two other modellers are known by name: an American, Mrs Patience Wright, who came to England in 1773, was said to be a spy, and made the effigy of William Pitt in 1779; and Miss Catherine Andras, 'modeller in wax to Queen Charlotte', who made Nelson's effigy in 1805.

Making effigies for state funerals could not, however, provide a regular income. A steadier living was to be made by modelling portraits of the living, or

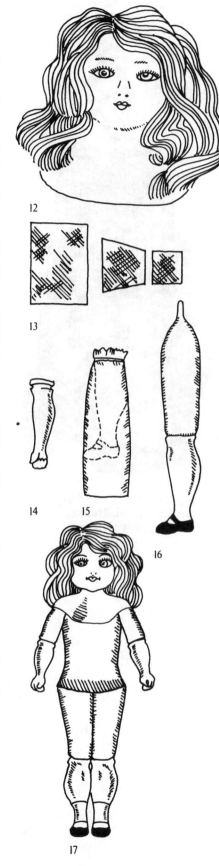

12 Finished head
13 Patterns for fabric body
14 Arm
15 Joining fabric with leg
16 Stuffed leg complete
17 Doll complete

191

English doll, 1770-80. Head, shoulders and hands of wax, *Victoria & Albert Museum*

by teaching the craft—as we learn from 18th century advertisements. A handbill dated 1711 tells us that a Mrs Salmon then exhibited her moving waxworks of the Royal Court of England: 140 figures as big as life. Mrs Salmon also sold 'all sorts of moulds and glass eyes' and taught 'the full art'.

Mrs Salmon died at the age of ninety in 1760—the year of Madame Tussaud's birth in France. By this time many fashionable ladies in England had taken up the pastime of dressing doll-like wax figures in elaborate costumes. Delicate and fragile, they were never intended for the tough handling of small children: perhaps they should be regarded as unconscious votive offerings to the goddesses of fashion.

In 1761 a doll was dressed by a member of the Powell family in an exact replica of her bridal dress; then, as each generation grew up, more doll brides joined the family collection. They are now housed in the Victoria and Albert Museum, the last bride having been made in 1902.

The wax doll trade

Between 1790 and 1935 thirty-six wax doll makers are listed in London street directories. Very few of the dolls they made, even if they survive in museums or private collections, bear any name or identification mark; but the expert eye can recognise with confidence the work of two outstanding families, the Pierottis and the Montanaris.

Domenico Pierotti, by trade a modeller in papier maché for fresques and ceiling decoration, left Italy and eventually, in 1780, settled in London. A decade or so later he was selling his wax dolls at a stall in the Pantheon Bazaar in Oxford Street. His son Enrico claimed to have invented a realistic baby doll modelled on Queen Victoria's first baby, the Princess Royal; and a newspaper advertisement gives a detailed list of the toys which could be bought at his shop, the Crystal Palace, which he opened in 1858 at 108 Oxford Street:

'H. Pierotti Gallery, London Crystal Palace, Oxford Street.

M. Pierotti respectfully informs his Patrons and the Public that he has considerably enlarged his stock, to which he has added new stock, in which will be found an extensive assortment of French and German Toys, Mediaeval Articles, Work Boxes, Rosewood French and German Toys, Rosewood Writing Desks, Dressing Cases etc.

My Juvenile Friends who to the Crystal Palace come,
And require a Sword, Violin, Trumpet or Drum,
A Shovel, a Barrow, a Rake or a Spade,
You'll find at our counter the best that are made;
The *New Eagle Kite*, with Traps, Balls and Bats,
German Boxes of Toys and Musical Cats,
The *Game* of *Aunt Sally* and English Farm,
And Pop-guns from France that will do you no harm;
To keep you in health 'tis my wish to contrive
The New Royal Game, that's called *Jack's Alive*.
Such beautiful dolls that will open their eyes,
You may wash, comb and dress them and not fear their cries;
The Game of "La Grace", Skipping Ropes, Plates and Dishes,
Battledores, Shuttlecocks, and Magnetic Fishes.
There's little black Topsy and Poor Uncle Tom,
A large Rocking Horse which you may ride on,
And at the year's end my young friends to please,
A profusion of goods for the *Christmas Trees*.
So dear little friends, just bear this in mind
'Tis at H. Pierotti's these wonders you'll find.'

Enrico's son and grandson, as we have seen, continued making wax dolls up to 1935.

At the Great Exhibition held in London's Hyde Park in 1851 only three

192

Robert, Marquis of Normanby
with his mother Catherine,
Duchess of Buckingham. Wax
figure from the Undercroft,
Westminster Abbey

193

Hornbook alphabet made into a gingerbread mould

English sampler with alphabet, 1643

British firms won prizes in the toy-making section, all the other prizewinners being French or German exhibitors. The British firm of A Bouchet had a representation of the Great Exhibition itself, with moving figures; while Spurin of Bond Street exhibited two mechanical models: one of a farmyard, the other of Gulliver in Lilliput.

The most remarkable and beautiful display of British-made toys in the exhibition was however that of Madame Augusta Montanari, who showed wax dolls dressed in a variety of costumes from a wide range of countries, arranged in 'family' groups. The Mexican group, for instance, comprised a street cobbler at work, a water carrier, a vegetable seller, and other native figures dancing. The intimate knowledge of Mexican Indian life these reveal has led some authorities to speculate that the Montanari family themselves may have originated not from Italy but from Latin America.

The techniques of wax doll making are relatively simple: an article in *Work: the Illustrated Weekly Journal of Handicrafts* for 20th November 1915 gives instructions for making a wax doll at home (wartime do-it-yourself!). A warm, liquid wax is poured into a water-saturated plaster mould, allowed to cool, and the excess wax drained off.

A doll's head made like this is rather fragile. It can be made a little stronger by pouring in a second coat of wax; but as this makes the head heavier the wax is sometimes reinforced in places by a layer of fine muslin, cheesecloth, or very thin papier maché. This was the process most used by the English doll makers.

Another, cheaper method is to make the doll's head of wood, papier maché or any other composition material and then dip it in wax to give a final finish to its complexion.

A third method, sometimes used for small dolls such as dolls' house dolls, or portrait dolls, is simply to carve a solid lump of wax, like a piece of wood, into a human likeness.

These techniques are mainly straightforward: the expertise lies in the original modelling (or carving), in the choosing of the wax and in the later processes of fitting the eyes, beautifying the face, and fixing the hair in place.

Learning and playing

Sugaring the pill—early teaching aids

Miss Campion, aged two and a half, was painted in 1661 demurely clutching a wooden bat. This was not a toy but a horn book—an early device for teaching children the letters of the alphabet. An inscribed sheet of parchment or paper was stuck to the wood, covered for protection with a transparent layer of horn, and given to the child to study. But high-spirited children would soon find ways of putting their hornbooks to more palatable uses; and by the 18th century, when supplies of paper were more plentiful and printed cardboard battledores replaced the hornbooks, their dual purpose was implicitly recognised. Alphabets were learned in the intervals between bouts of shuttlecock whacking.

Meanwhile, however, a new raw material on the market was making, for the luckier Tudor and Stuart children, the job of learning their letters an even sweeter one. Cane sugar, though the Crusaders had tasted it, remained an expensive and little known luxury until Christopher Columbus planted the first sugar canes in the Antilles. But by a century later, in 1627, when eighty English settlers were harvesting sugar in Barbados, a new and vastly profitable industry had come to fruition—at a cost of misery to untold thousands of Africans rounded up and transported as slave labour to the Indies.

The new sweetmeats could be disastrous for their consumers also. Queen Elizabeth's teeth were blackened and rotted by her indulgence in them; and toothache became a commoner complaint than ever before. But what was that to a Tudor child if now and again he could get hold of a nibble of marzipan, a comfit to suck, a candied rose petal, a preserved or jellied fruit to savour?

194

A ready way for children to learn their A.B.C.

CAuse 4 large dice of bone or wood to be made, and upon every square, one of the small letters of the cross row to be graven, but in some bigger shape, and the child using to play much with them,

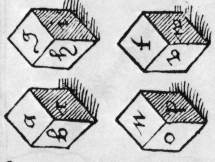

and being always told what letter chanceth, will soon gain his Alphabet, as it were by the way of sport or pastime. I have heard of a pair of cards, whereon most of the principall Grammer rules have been printed, and the School-Master hath found good sport thereat with his schollers.

From AT Tuer's *History of the Horn Book*: 'A ready way for children to learn their ABC'.

Left: Miss Campion holding a horn book

Elizabethan wooden horn book

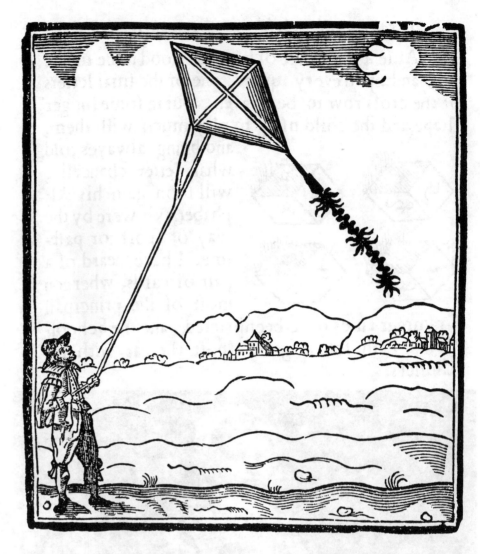

As sugar became more easily available than honey, bakers could increase their output of cakes of all kinds. Great slabs of gingerbread, baked with the letters of the alphabet on them, were sold at country fairs; and a child might get a piece for every letter he recognised:

'The bakers, to increase their trade,
Made alphabets of gingerbread;
That folks might swallow what they read,
All the letters were digested,
Hateful ignorance detested.'

Little girls would also painlessly absorb their ABC while learning how to sew. Samplers, originally simply records of sewing patterns to be copied, came to be used first as vehicles for teaching techniques of sewing they would need when they were grown up; then as a means of instruction in the alphabet and, through map samplers, in geography; and only later to record family joys and sorrows and to inculcate moral virtues and submission to the will of God.

Burton's catalogue of recreations

How merry was the 'Merrie England of Elizabethan and early Stuart times? We cannot tell. Certainly for most life was ill-nourished and very insecure by comparison with today. Yet it is hard to escape the impression that it was more full-blooded. And its range of pleasures surely bears comparison with today's.

The most comprehensive review of the recreations available to the 17th century Englishman is provided, ironically, by Burton in his *Anatomy of Melancholy*:

196

'Cards, dice, hawkes and hounds are rocks upon which men lose themselves, when they are imprudently handled, and beyond their fortunes . . . Hunting and hawking are honest recreations, and fit for some great men, but not for every base inferior person . . . Ringing, bowling, shooting, playing with keel-pins, tronks, coits, pitching of bars, hurling, wrestling, leaping, running, fencing, mustering, swimming, playing with wasters, foils, foot-balls, balowns, running at the quintain, and the like, are the common recreations of country folks; riding of great horses, running at rings, tilts, and tournaments, horse races, and wild goose chases, which are disports of greater men, and good in themselves, though many gentlemen by such means gallop quite out of their fortunes.'

Pastimes Burton lists as common both in town and country include 'bull-baitings and bear-baitings, dancers on ropes, jugglers, comedies, tragedies, artillery gardens, and cock-fighting', while among ordinary recreations in winter are 'cards, tables, dice, shovelboards, chess-play, the philosopher's game, small trunks, shuttlecock, billiards, music, masks, singing, dancing, ulegames, frolicks, jests, riddles, catches, cross purposes, questions and commands, merry tales of errant knights, queens, lovers, lords, ladies, giants, dwarfs, thieves, cheaters, witches, fairies, goblins, and friars'.

'Let the common people', Burton concludes, 'freely feast, sing, dance, have puppet-plays, hobby-horses, tabers, crowds, and bag-pipes; let them play at ball and barley-brakes. Plays, masks, jesters, gladiators, tumblers, and jugglers are to be winked at, lest the people should do worse than attend them'.

Football

To trace in more detail the history of most of these recreations would be tedious; but football, as the paragon of popular sports to-day, deserves more than a passing mention. It was already widespread enough by the 14th century to incur royal displeasure and be banned by public edict—apparently because it was thought to impede the progress of archery. Similar bans were repeated from time to time over the next 300 years, but to temporary effect only, if that.

Barclay's *Ship of Fools*, published in 1508, pictures football as a sport for tough countrymen:

> 'The sturdie plowman, lustie, strong and bold,
> Overcometh the winter with driving the foote-ball,
> Forgetting labour and many a grievous fall;'

and records that country boys, since leather was precious, simply used a blown-up bladder, which they stuffed with peas and beans (they also used hands as generously as feet in those days):

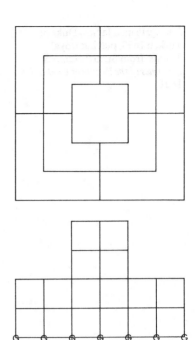

Nine Men's Morris and Fox & Geese

Below: Blowing up a football

197

'And nowe in the winter, when men kill the fat swine,
They get the bladder and blow it great and thin,
With many beans and peason put within;
It ratleth, soundeth, and shineth clere and fayre,
While it is thrown and caste up in the ayre,
Eche one contendeth and hath a great delighte
With foote and with hande the bladder for to smite;
If it fall to the grounde, they lifte it up agayne,
And this way to labour they count it no payne.'

Contrast with this idyllic picture Sir Thomas Elyot a couple of decades later, for whom football is 'nothyng but beastely fury and extreme violence' and Stubbes, whose *Anatomie of Abuses* (1583) describes it as 'a devilishe pastime . . ., whereof groweth envy, rancour and malice, and great effusion of blood, as experience daily teacheth'.

But not everywhere, surely? Readers with experience of mixed hockey may doubt whether in Tudor football the female of the species was less deadly than the male; yet Sir Philip Sidney's Dialogue between two Shepherds, as Strutt who quotes it in his *Sports and Pastimes of the People of England* comments, does evoke a gentler scene, more reminiscent of Nausicaa and her handmaidens:

'A time there is for all, my mother often says,
When she, with skirts tucked very high,
With girls at football plays.'

Meanwhile, football had spread to the towns, reinforcing the objectors' protests. Thus Davenant writes of London in 1634:

'I would now make a safe retreat, but that methinks I am stopped by one of your heroic games called football; which I conceive not very conveniently civil in the streets, especially in such irregular and narrow roads as Crooked Lane. Yet it argues your courage, much like your military pastime of throwing at cocks, since you have long allowed these two valiant exercises in the streets.' One is left with an engaging uncertainty whether our courage consists in our willingness to run the gauntlet of these disturbances, or whether Davenant was ascribing to Crooked Lane the role later attributed to the playing fields of Eton.

James I's advice to his son

James I's *Basilikon Doron,* his personal catalogue of the activities appropriate to the training of an heir to the throne, puts football firmly outside the pale, but is almost as severe on, of all pastimes, chess:

'Bodily exercises are very commendable, as well for banishing of idleness . . . as for making the body able and durable for travell. But from the court I debarre all rough and violent exercises: as the foote-ball, meeter for lameing than for making able the users thereof; and likewise such tumbling tricks as only serve for comoedians and balladines to win their bread with: but the exercises I would have you to use, although but moderately, . . . are running, leaping, wrestling, fencing, dancing and playing at the caitch, or tennise, archerie, palle-malle, and other such fair and pleasant field games . . .

'As for sitting, or house pastimes, . . . I will not agree with the curiositie of some learned men of our age in forbidding cardes, dice, and such like games of hazard: when it is foule and stormie weather, then I say may ye lawfully play at the cardes or tables; for as to diceing, I think it becometh best deboshed souldiers to play at on the heads of their drums, being only ruled by hazard, and subject to knavish cogging; and as for the chesse, I think it over-fond, because it is overwise and philosophicke a folly.'

Chess a folly? Chess over-fond? Chess, which Bishop Aethric—so history relates—found King Canute the Dane absorbed in when he visited him at midnight on an important mission? It is time to turn our backs on such philistine sophistication, to explore the Middle and darker Ages.

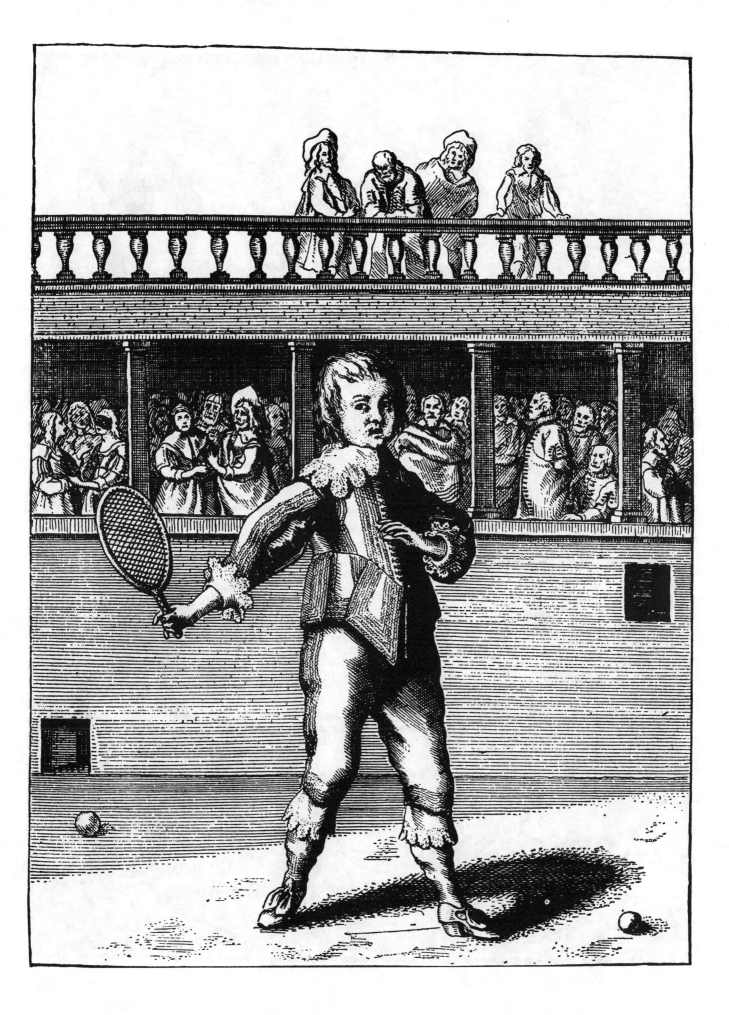

The Middle Ages

As we move back through the centuries the record of individual playthings thins out almost to disappearance, and cannot, even if it were preserved, have been considerable. For if the Renaissance spells the emancipation, in a measure, of individual genius, the Middle Ages by contrast reflect a society whose achievements were the cooperative work of communities—in the building of cathedrals, the formation of the guilds, the organisation (however imperfect) of feudal and of monastic life. And when we think of recreation in the Middle Ages, we think first of the pageants, processions and fairs liberally scattered through the calendar, to which ordinary people would come in their hundreds—men, women and children together, released for a while, most of them, from monotonous and perhaps solitary drudgery.

Bartholomew Fair, then, which we have visited in Ben Jonson's time, can appropriately set the scene for us of Londoners at leisure over four hundred years earlier. Our guide is William Fitzstephen, clerk and sub-deacon to Thomas à Becket, who wrote a description of London in 1174. By good fortune a monk of the Priory of St. Bartholomew illustrated, a few years later, a book of Decretals with sketches of contemporary life; and Henry Morley, in his *Memoirs of Bartholomew Fair* published in 1874, has happily conjoined the two sources.

The annual Fair was in early September, but Smithfield, where it was held, was an open space inviting to recreation the whole year round. Thus we read that on Shrove Tuesday every boy took to school his fighting cock, and 'they spent all the morning in watching their cocks fight in the schoolroom. After dinner all the youth went into the fields to play the well-known game of ball' ('ludum pilae celebrem' in Fitzstephen's Latin—probably hand-ball rather than football). On Sundays in Lent troops of young men charged out of the gates with lances and shields to engage in sham fights. While in the Easter holidays 'they counterfeit a Sea Fight: a Pole is set up in the middle of the River, with a Target well fastened thereon, and a young Man stands in a Boat which is rowed with Oars, and driven on with the Tide, who with his Spear hits the Target in his Passage: with which Blow, if he break the Spear and stand upright, so that he hold Footing, he hath his Desire: but, if his Spear continue unbroken by the Blow, he is tumbled into the Water, and his Boat passeth clear away'.

On summer evenings the youth would run, leap, wrestle, cast the stone, or contend with hucklers, swords and arrows while maidens danced to the tabor by moonlight. These sports natural to Smithfield must have been among the recreations sought on the great Smithfield holiday provided by the Fair.

From John Morley's *Memoirs of Bartholomew Fair*, 1874

Facing: From a MS in the Bodleian Library

201

Handball

The 'famous game of ball' which the scholars played on Shrove Tuesday had, of course, a long ancestry. Joseph Strutt, placing Nausicaa firmly in Corcyra (the modern Corfu), cites the Odyssey in Pope's translation:

> 'O'er the green mead the sporting virgins play,
> Their shining veils unbound; along the skies,
> Tost and retost, the ball incessant flies.'

In mediaeval France the game was known as 'pila palmaria'—the 'jeu de paume'; in England as hand-ball.

In Tudor times hand-ball begins to develop into the modern game of fives: a padded glove is worn. In 1591 Queen Elizabeth, entertained at a nobleman's house in Hampshire, watched while ten servants 'squared out the forme of a tennis-court . . . and played five to five with handball at bard and cord as they tearme it'. Fives, like tennis, required an enclosed space; hence the popularity of churchyards. In the Basque country the 'jeu de paume' is still played against church walls; at Eton College, because it was evolved between the buttresses on the north wall of the chapel, it acquired quite individual characteristics, still preserved.

Above and facing: from a MS in the Bodleian Library

Tennis

Tennis, like handball, had mediaeval ancestry: French in origin, it was rapidly domesticated in England. Some, according to Strutt, derive its name from the expression 'Tenez le jeu'; others from 'tennes', on the analogy of 'fives' but representing the count of two opposing teams instead of one only. Literary references date from the 14th century: thus, Troilus in Chaucer's *Troilus and Cryseyde* (1380) chides Pandarus with fickleness by comparing him to the to-and-fro motion of a racket. Holinshed's account of the French Dauphin's gift of tennis balls to Henry V gives Shakespeare a good springboard:

> 'When we have matched our rackets to these balls,
> We will in France, by God's grace, play a set
> Shall strike his father's crown into the hazard.'

By the end of the 15th century tennis was quite big business. There is a record of the Ironmongers' Company selling to Thos. Cook in Edward IV's reign forty-seven gross of tennis balls (the company probably owned a court in Fenchurch Street). Henry VII and VIII both played in a number of courts in London and the home counties (one at Windsor was still standing in 1607, though roofless); and authority to set up a court was eagerly sought after.

As with football, repeated bans were imposed on the common people's playing, since the need for an enclosed space led to unsuitable places being chosen. As early as 1447 the Bishop of Exeter was complaining of young people during divine service playing at unlawful games in the cloister such as 'the

Monumental effigy to John Stanley in the church of Elford, near Lichfield. He was killed by a tennis ball. Illustration from Strutt

toppe, penny prykke, and most atte tenys', defiling walls and breaking windows. Tennis, therefore, was confined to the courtyards of great houses, or such was the intention. The peculiarities of the modern court (the 'grille' and so on) no doubt derive from its features being copied from a particular courtyard having certain irregularities.

Hockey and golf

These games too have pre-Tudor origins. Hockey, like tennis, seems to have been a derivative of hand-ball. The mediaeval game of hurling, though played without sticks, certainly has an affinity with hockey; and by the early 16th century we find references to hockey sticks or staves.

Golf in its early forms is barely distinguishable from hockey: both were 'bandy-ball' because of the shape of the stick. But in the 15th century it developed as Scotland's national game (it had all the space it needed there), and soon spread south. It was fashionable among the nobility in the early 17th century: James I's son played, so did Charles I; while James II used a 'fore-caddie'. As early as the 1750s there was a club at Pau in the south of France, apparently so much appreciated by the British military set that they caused similar clubs to be set up in England at Westward Ho! and other choice locations. Pau was later a favourite course of Edward VIII's.

Skating

Skating could well be of prehistoric origin, as it owes its invention primarily to necessity, especially for the Dutch from whom the word derives. Fitzstephen describes how 'when that great moor which washed Moorfields, at the north wall of the city, is frozen over, great companies of young men go to sport upon the ice; and bind to their shoes bones, as the legs of some beasts; and hold stakes in their hands, headed with sharp iron, which sometimes they stick against the ice; and these men go on with speed, as doth a bird in the air, or darts shot from some warlike engine. Some times two men set themselves at a distance and run one against another, as it were at tilt, with these stakes, wherewith one or both parties are thrown down, not without some hurt to their bodies . . .

'Others' (younger ones no doubt) 'make a sheet of ice as large as a millstone; and having placed one of their companions upon it, they draw him along, while it sometimes happens that moving in slippery places they all fall headlong.' It sounds more fun than the murderous 'tilting'.

England shared, of course, with other countries the pleasure of most sedentary games: diceing, cards, chess or whatever. But virtually none of these owe to Britain either their origins or their distinctive developed characteristics. The ball games whose early history we have adumbrated are, by contrast, a British gift to the world in their developed form. For it was in Britain that the rules of football, cricket and other team games were codified; and it was in the British 'public' boarding schools of the 19th century that liberal open space, lusty adolescence, and the cult of physical prowess and team rivalry combined to nurture them. It was Britain's industrial supremacy, too, which allowed her to take the lead in legalising 'Saturday afternoon off', so opening the way for football's pre-eminence as the sport of the people—first as participants, increasingly as spectators, outstandingly as gamblers.

From a MS in the Bodleian Library

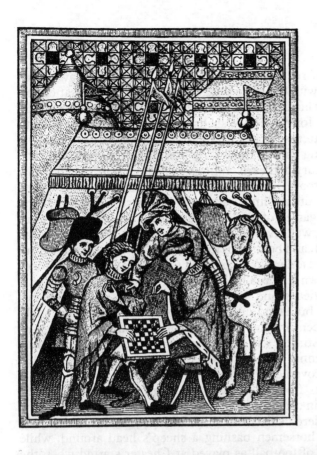

'Tables', a form of backgammon. Illustration from Strutt

Left: Medieval knights playing chess. Illustration from Strutt and chess pieces of walrus ivory found in the Isle of Lewis, 12th century, *British Museum*

Below: From a MS in the British Library

Pottery money-box, medieval, excavated in London, *British Museum*

Below: Knucklebones, a natural toy from the beginning of time. The girls at play drawn by Rachel Waller after a Pompeian frieze

First toys

What did the children of our remotest ancestors play with as they crawled out into the daylight? Probably with the same things as readily attract the attention of small babies today, if they have the luck to come by them: a little bone or twig to grasp and bite; a seedpod for rattle; two shells interlocked; pretty pebbles to pick up and arrange into patterns, or roll like marbles. Rattles to calm a baby's cries, to scare away marauding wild beasts, to frighten evil spirits lurking in the dark; even elegant 18th century and early 19th century silver rattles ended in a length of coral, or a wolf's tooth—traditional charms against the evil eye.

Pebbles, fruit stones, or nuts of similar shape and colour, lined up in rows, would become counters in games of skill and foresight. Knucklebones from sheep or other large animals, well chewed and dried in the sun, would be thrown in the air, caught in the hand, and because of their irregular shape used as a form of dice. The same animal's bladder would be used to store fat or to carry food; but it would also serve, blown up, as a ball. A leather covering would make it stronger: a bit of sheepskin tied round it with the wool inside, and it could not only be thrown and caught, but stand up to hitting with any convenient stick. Indeed, until the late 17th century the balls used for the game of royal tennis were made from sheepskin stuffed with hair. Gradually cotton replaced hair, until a century later royal tennis balls were being made from strips of woollen material tightly rolled and covered by white Melton cloth.

Ingenuity can create balls from the most varied materials: tightly woven grasses, reeds and rushes; thin cane, as they are still made in Thailand to-day; or silk waste inside an embroidered silk covering, as in Japan. It is said that polo was originated by Mongol horsemen bashing a sheep's head around; while legend has it that the game of football as played at Chester started when the locals dribbled up the field a captured Dane's head.

But it was no doubt the sheer tedium of many jobs, rather than dramatic events such as these, which over the centuries spurred the young to invent new pastimes. The boredom of long hours spent minding the sheep or taking the cows out to grass would give young lads the world over time to evolve games of gradually increasing elaboration: whacking stones, then balls—with sticks, then with crooks; then setting up three-legged milking stools as wickets, or stakes as goal posts, and developing the rudiments of games later to be known as golf, cricket, hockey. While as for the traditional ceremonial games associated with the changing seasons, such as beating the bounds of your parish—these have their phantom origin behind the mists of time, in pre-Christian rituals marking the death of the old year and the birth of the new . . .

Reed pipes

Left: Natural toys: shells, pebbles, gourds

Bibliography

Chapter I
Buhler, Michael, *Tin Toys,* Bergstrom & Boyle Books, London, 197
& S Harley, Basil, *Toy Shop Steam,* Angus Books, London, 1978.
Pressland, David, *The Art of the Tin Toy* New Cavendish Books, London, 1976.

Chapter II
Rodaway, Angela, *A London Childhood,* Batsford, London, 1960.
Randall, Peter, *The Products of Binns Road,* New Cavendish Books, London, 1977.

Chapter III
Bull, Peter, *Bear with Me,* Hutchinson, London, 1969.
Gould, MP, *Frank Hornby,* New Cavendish Books—reprint of 1915 edition.
Hutchings, Margaret, *The Book of the Teddy Bear,* Mills & Boon, London, 1964.
Shears, Sarah, *Tapioca for Tea,* Elek Books, London, 1971.

Chapter IV
Acland, Eleanor, *Goodbye for the Present* Hodder & Stoughton, London, 1935.
Allen, Thomas, *History and Antiquities of London,* George Virtue, London, 1837.
Burnett, John (ed.), *Useful Toil: Autobiographies of Working People 1820-1920,* Allen Lane, London, 1974, and Pelican, London 1977.
Douglas, Norman, *London Street Games,* St Catherine Press, London, 1916.
Garratt, John, *Collecting Model Soldiers,* David & Charles, Newton Abbot, 1975.
Greene, Vivien, *English Dolls' Houses,* Batsford, London, 1958.
Hindley, Charles, *Life and Times of James Catnach,* (compiled by) Reeves and Turner, London, 1869.
Horne, Richard Henry, *Memoirs of a London Doll* 1846, reprint—André Deutsch, London, 1967.
Landells, E, *The Girl's Own Toy Maker,* Griffith & Farran, London, 1863.
Lane, Margaret, *The Tale of Beatrix Potter,* Frederick Warne, London, 1946.
Latham, Jean, *Dolls' Houses,* A & C Black, London, 1969.
Leech, John, *Young Troublesome,* Bradbury & Evans, London, 1850
Low, Frances, *Queen Victoria's Dolls,* George Newnes, London, 1894.
Mayhew, Henry, *Articles in the 'Morning Chronicle',* London, 1851.
Rees, Goronwy, *A History of Marks and Spencer,* Weidenfeld and Nicolson, London, 1969.
Roe, Gordon, *The Victorian Child,* Phoenix House, 1959.
Speaight, George, *Juvenile Drama,* Macdonald, London, 1946; revised & reprinted as *The History of the English Toy Theatre,* Studio Vista, London, 1969.
Stanley, Dorothy, *Street Arabs,* Cassell & Co, London, 1890.
Wells, HG, *Floor Games,* Dent & Son, London, 1913.
Wells, HG, *Little Wars,* Quantum Reprints, London, 1966.
Wilson, AE, *Penny Plain and Twopence Coloured,* Harrap, London, 1932.

Chapter V
Bell, RC, *Board & Table Games,* Oxford University Press, London, 1960.
Dodsley, Robert, *The Toy Shop,* Vol 3. 1784 Bell's British Theatre, 1735.
Early, Alice, *English Dolls, Effigies and Puppets,* Batsford, London, 1955.
Hannas, Linda, *The English Jigsaw Puzzle,* Wayland, London, 1972.
Heal, Ambrose, *London's Tradesmans' Cards of the 18th Century,* Batsford, London, 1925.
Muir, Percy, *English Children's Books,* Batsford, London, 1954.
Paget-Hett, Frances (ed.), *The Memoirs of Susan Sibbald, 1783-1812,* John Lane, 1926.
Pinto, EH, *Treen,* G Bell & Sons, London, 1969.
Pinto, EH & EP, *Tunbridge & Scottish & Souvenir Woodware,* Batsford, London, 1970

Tuer, A, *Old Fashioned Children's Books*, Leadenhall Press, London, 1899.

Tuer, A, *Pages and Pictures from Forgotten Children's Books*, Leadenhall Press, London, 1898.

Whitehouse, FRB, *Table Games of Georgian and Victorian Days*, Priory Press, Toyston, 1951.

Chapter VI

Besant, Walter, *A Survey of London*, A & C Black, London, 1902.

Ewing, Elizabeth, *History of Children's Costume*, Batsford, London, 1977.

Gerken, Jo, *Wonderful Dolls of Wax*, Doll Research Associates, Nebraska, 1964.

Jonson, Ben, *Bartholomew Fair 1614*, Penguin Books, London, 1966.

Lynd, Sylvia, *English Children*, William Collins, London, 1942.

Morley, Henry, *Memoirs of Bartholomew Fair*, J Routledge, (4th edition) Glasgow, 1892.

Power, Rhoda and Eileen, *Boys and Girls of History*, Cambridge University Press, 1942.

Seaton, M, *Sweets*, Exhibition Catalogue, Whitechapel Gallery, London, 1973.

Stuart, Dorothy, *The Young Londoner through the Ages*, Harrap, London, 1962.

Strutt, J, *Sports and Pastimes of the People of England*, Methuen, (reprint), London, 1903.

General—Dolls

Boehn, Max von, *Dolls and Puppets*, Cooper Square, (reprint), New York, 1966.

Coleman, Dorothy, Elizabeth and Evelyn, *The Collector's Encyclopedia of Dolls*, Robert Hale, London, 1977.

Desmonde, Kay, *Dolls and Dolls' Houses*, Letts, London, 1972.

Fox, Carl, *The Doll*, Abrams, New York, 1974.

Fraser, Antonia, *Dolls*, Weidenfeld and Nicolson, London, 1963.

Hart, Luella, *Directory of British Dolls*, USA, 1964.

Hillier, Mary, *Dolls and Dollmakers*, Weidenfeld and Nicolson, London, 1968.

Hillier, Mary (Ed.), *Pollock's Dictionary of English Dolls*, Ernest Benn, London, 1980.

Jacob, Flora Gill and Fauholt, Estrid, *Dolls and Dolls' Houses*, Charles Tuttle, New York & Tokyo, 1967.

King, Constance Eileen, *The Collector's History of Dolls*, Robert Hale, London, 1977.

Mathes, Ruth, *Decline and Fall of the Wooden Doll*, Doll Collector's Manual, 1964.

Noble, John, *Dolls*, Studio Vista, London, 1967.

St George, Eleanor, *Dolls of Three Centuries*, Chas. Scribner's Sons, New York, 1951.

White, Gwen, *European and American Dolls*, Batsford, London, 1966.

General—Toys

Ayres, James, *British Folk Art*, Barrie & Jackson, London, 1977.

Cadbury, Betty, *Playthings Past*, David & Charles, Newton Abbot, Devon, 1976.

Culff, Robert, *The World of Toys*, Paul Hamlyn, London, 1969.

Daiken, Leslie, *Children's Toys through the Ages*, Batsford, London, 1952.

Flick, Pauline, *Discovering Toys and Toy Museums*, Shire Publications, 1971.

Fraser, Antonia, *A History of Toys*, Weidenfeld and Nicolson, London, 1966.

Gordon, Leslie, *Peepshow into Paradise*, London, 1953.

Heard, James and Burke, Jenny (Eds.) *Pollock's World of Toys*, Pollock's Toy Museum, London

Hillier, Mary, *Automata and Mechanical Toys*, Jupiter Books, London, 1976.

Hillier, Mary, *A Pageant of Toys*, Elek Books, London, 1976.

King, Constance Eileen, *Toys and Dolls for Collectors*, Hamlyn, London, 1973.

Murray, Patrick, *Toys*, Studio Vista, London, 1968.

White, Gwen, *Toys, Dolls, Automata: Marks and Labels*, Batsford, London, 1975.

Antique Toys & Their Background, Batsford, London, 1971.

Index

Notes:

1.   Types of doll and toy are indexed under 'doll' and 'toy' respectively.
     Dolls and toys with trade names are indexed under the trade name.
2.   Books, magazines and newspapers are in inverted commas.
3.   A reference in italics indicates that an illustration only is referred to, not the main text.